Praise for *In the Jaws of the Black Dogs*

"One of the most spiritual, life-affirming books in Canadian literature."
The Gazette (Montreal)

"To accompany Mays on his life quest is to feast on his ruminations on each phase—in chronological order, father fixation, Christian faith, healing psychotherapy, 60s radicalism, intellectual enlightenment, ambiguous sexuality, abiding spousal love, art, alcoholism, Christian faith (more deeply), Prozac and gardening.... Brave and lucid, often profound...one of the best books I've read this year."
NOW Magazine (Toronto)

"Brilliant...simultaneously achingly painful and movingly insightful...breathtakingly honest and relentlessly self-analytical... Fortunately for us all, so far, despite his seductive waltz with suicide, Bentley Mays has lived to tell the tale—and to tell it better than anyone else I have encountered."
The Edmonton Journal

"Brave and harrowing...as honest and informative an account as one could imagine."
Sunday Free Press (Brandon)

"Tackles the complexities of depression's origins—the mysterious mind-brain relationship, the complex debates of drugs versus psychotherapy—with the nuance and intelligence they deserve."
The Globe and Mail

"*In the Jaws of the Black Dogs* is not a book about depression; it is depression experienced and confronted."
The Hamilton Spectator

"Is *In the Jaws of the Black Dogs* a depressing book? Not in the least. It is a moving book, a powerful book, which provides real insight.... That Mays has survived at all...may be attributed to his three saving graces: his faith, his love of art, and the love of a strong woman with a hot temper, who forced him to do something with his life.... This is not a self-help book; which is precisely why depressives and the people who love them may find it so helpful."

Quill & Quire

"Mays emerges as a man with much backbone and courage as well as a first rate journalist. He has learned to live and work around his depression, and what he relates about the conditions under which he works makes *In the Jaws of the Black Dogs* one of the most memorable stories I have encountered this year."

Northern Daily News

"A rare first-person account by a man who has risen to the top of his profession and had a family while coping with his disorder."

The Daily News (Halifax)

IN THE JAWS
OF THE
BLACK DOGS

A Memoir of Depression

IN THE JAWS

OF THE

BLACK DOGS

JOHN BENTLEY MAYS

HarperCollinsPublishers

FIRST U.S. EDITION

Library of Congress Cataloging-in-Publication Data

Mays, John Bentley.
    In the jaws of the black dogs : a memoir of
depression / John Bentley Mays.
       p. cm.
    ISBN 0-06-019288-7
    1. Mays, John Bentley — Mental health.
    2. Depression, Mental — Patients — Biography. I. Title
RC537.M3923 1999
616.85'27'0092 B—dc21   99-22461

99 00 01 02 03 RRD 10 9 8 7 6 5 4 3 2 1

to Stephen Godfrey

who will not read it

Contents

Writing Depression

*T**his*** book is a life with the black dogs of depression.
I have written it in a clearing bounded by thickets
roamed by the killing dogs, sometimes wondering, in the
writing, whether I would complete it before they returned on
silent paws to snatch the text and me away. For the depressed can
never be sure we can finish anything we begin, or indeed certain
of anything, except the black dogs' eventual return, and their terrible circling at the clearing's edge.

They arrive at times that bewilder people unfamiliar with
their ways. It may be on a shy morning early in spring, when

breezes bear fragrant hints of new stirrings, the winter's ending. It can be in those wonderful weeks when the first garden shoots are shouldering aside dirt and crusts of grimy snow, and thrusting up to blossom in the cold air. The dogs may come back just when we've hit our stride at a favourite game; or almost finished the assignment that will round out a career, or fulfil a dream; or as erotic excitement or the sound of far desire is interrupting life's monotonous score.

The black dogs may also come back disguised as bearers of familiar misery—after an ordinary failure, or a social blunder, or during a prolonged period of indecision. After all, the chronically depressed are vulnerable to the same slights, neglects, sufferings and losses, frustrations, hard times and rages as the rest of humankind. I, too, have known grief of the sort shared by all the living who have lost or been betrayed by one deeply loved.

But we know other things the undepressed do not know, except at a distance, or in the distorting mirror of language. This is a book of such things: the sudden scattering of thought without prompt or warning, the abrupt turning of abundant fields into deserts, the theft of desire and compassion—the shedding of tears that do not heal, agony without ground or end or explanation, without point or worth.

This is also a book of desire, of wishing to belong to the weeping, rejoicing humanity around me—and of knowing the punishments meted out by the black dogs to the depressed who want such fulfilment. Love has been offered to me again and again; and I've felt an answering love inside me flicker and quicken, only to flare up as desolating hate against the offerer of love. I have felt boredom and envy seize my depressed soul during a celebration of another's joy—and at such moments I have preferred death to yet another banishment into isolation in the midst of happiness.

There are a great many books about depression. This is not one of them. It is pain *written*, not *observed*; a depressive writer's writing, a testament transcribed from wounded flesh to paper in the clearing, before the black dogs' inevitable return.

Paging back through diaries kept over the last thirty years, I do not find it difficult to spot the moments in which the dogs have begun their drastic circling. They are points at which a certain lying begins to emerge in the routine weft and weave of diarizing. At first, these new lies are little, just so many plausible minor blamings for the first irregularities in life's predictable rhythms, the first cracks in the ring of social rituals.

If I woke up with the familiar lethargy, and could not pull myself out of bed and get dressed until noon, or spent an afternoon crying the scant, drizzling tears peculiar to depression—here's the lie—it was just the doleful sound of winter rain blowing against the window-panes, or the bitter, unremitting cold that sometimes comes in February. When the weather was glorious, some other cause came quickly to mind. (A lifetime of depression makes one remarkably resourceful in this unpleasant way.)

Fickle weathers, of course, had nothing to do with the drawing near of such thoughts. Bad weather makes many sane and reasonable people feel low—but perhaps because I am not entirely reasonable, I am not a person so affected. When not stirring the simmering pot of lies within, I find much to love in the coldest days of deep winter—the brilliance of the lobelia-blue skies, the pale silken sunshine falling gently through the skylights on pots of blooming white narcissus, warming the air with its naïve sweetness. Apart from heavy summer thunderstorms, I love most the cold rains of autumn and spring.

But on the mornings of the nearing of my silent, ancient enemy, I forget all that, and blame what is close at hand; even weather I would otherwise find delightful. Thoughts of worthlessness whirl inside my head, casting out all happier thoughts; and one thing after another slips out of my control. The bills are not paid, the garbage not taken out, the book lies unread beside my chair, the article is unwritten. And there come upon me those afflictions I blame everything *but* depression for: the rasping dryness of spirit, crippled awareness of whatever is lovely and kindly, exhaustion lingering and irremediable. And, worst of all, the after-image burned into my eyes by the nearness of the dogs, the vision of myself as waste and ruin.

Undone things begin to build up around my legs like silt, becoming a thick sediment of undoing, unworthiness to do. The repulsive sedimentation continues, the exhaustion and paralysis becomes intractable, and I find myself immobilized in the rock boot of consolidated bile.

———

The lies—*it's just the weather, it's just the time of year*—are confined to my diaries and to my private musings, long after the symptoms become public. There is no point in lying to my wife or my friends, who are too familiar with the signs to be deceived. Because they loathe this disorder, what it has done to them and to me, they will not listen with kindly patience to my groundless blaming. So I write; or, rather, depression *writes me*: each tear, a letter; each word in the demonic litany of self-hatred, an excerpt from a vocabulary of hell that is probably as old as the world.

Then comes the end of lies, and of self-hatred and self-reproach; then comes the final approach of the black dogs. The lies stop. Or, to be more precise, the *melodrama* stops, the creaking old-fashioned lying of the language. All that gives way to a new, emotionless "objectivity." I sense myself as meat.

In precise diary entries, depression's return is finally and frankly acknowledged. The intensifying symptoms are listed, occasionally with a slight peppering of the old complaining commentary, more usually without it. The list is always the same: weariness, exhaustion, a sharply decreased ability to concentrate, to gather my wits for the execution of the simplest jobs; the headaches, the annulment of joy, purpose. Yet the forensic language I invoke springs from nothing in my own heart or mind, is no more original than my routine complaining. Rather, it slides down on the page out of clinical case histories and medical records, a portrait of the *nobody*, nameless, extinguished, who is the topic of the technical literature on depression.

I have read the literature that now provides me with terms of order, pretending to study the technical language of depression—but really studying the way of looking, of writing, embodied in such texts. It is a poetry of the scalpel's quick slash, the spurt and stanching of blood, clamping back successive layers of skin, fat, muscle, the probe with a point of gleaming metal of the nothingness at the centre. Writing myself up as *case*, I experience myself, pleasurably, obscenely, as object. The former exacerbation of subjectivity is gone, now that the cyst known as *soul* is lanced, and all that remains is flesh, killed by the invasion of medical power, stiffening, cooling.

Of all we say, I suspect the undepressed find our peaceful talk of death most difficult to understand. Writing now within the circle of another kind of peace—and though I have known it well—I find the recollection of that dark blessedness hard. But this much I recall: how everything seems to be so much despicable trickery—music and art, the beauties of roadside wildflowers or of blue wintry skies, the smell of damp, warming earth in a spring thaw. Perhaps death loses all loathsomeness when the only other option is self-hatred, the waste of time in tears, regret, isolation.

So it is that, unless the black dogs withdraw—as they often do, mysteriously, leaving us drained of moral force and psychic energy—a kind of dark blessedness can germinate in the mind's loam, now moist with the sweet liquid fantasies of death.

Not all depressives are offered this perfect resignation by the black dogs, their last gift before they murder us, using our own hands. I have known this pacific calm only a few times. But when it came, a certain quiet gradually dawned, and all fears of suicide's pain and violence faded like mist before a new day's sun.

My thoughts were suffused with prospects of the endless peace lying beyond what now seemed a very little disruption, the slight, almost painless gash or step needed to bear me into that absolute and peaceful nothingness.

The howling pain hounding me into disarray and hideous embarrassment was gone. All within me was clear, calm, and focused on the minute preparations for suicide. What remained, as Michel Foucault has written, was to "decorate it, arrange the details, find the ingredients, imagine it, choose it, get advice on it, shape it into a work without spectators, one which exists only for oneself just for that shortest little moment of life."

A Yiddish proverb warns: *Beware of silent water, a silent dog, and a silent enemy.*

The advice is excellent, if impractical. Depression dwells in dark and silence, and for that very reason we can neither sense it nor avoid it. It lurks in the fabric and deep structures of language, creating what may appear to be a variant of ordinary life, but is not. Depression is "*another* life," the French psychoanalyst Julia Kristeva has written. If parallel to the ordinary experiencing and surviving of other people, it is merely a simulation, "unlivable, heavy with daily sorrows, tears held back or shed, a total despair, scorching at times, then wan and empty...a devitalized existence that, although occasionally fired by the effort I make to prolong it, is ready at any moment for a plunge into death."

If a life unlike any other, it is also a malignancy unlike others, never showing itself in eruptions, fleshly corruptions, physical weakenings. It does not kill directly by, say, ruining a vital organ; it does not permanently disfigure the face, or wreak havoc on a gland or tube a surgeon can see. Though the psychiatrists insist on discussing it as a malignancy, depression cannot be removed, or targeted for treatment with fire, poison or the knife. Unlike a diseased liver or a stomach tumour, it has no weight; like the vampire, it casts no shadow.

Or at least it is shadowless until thickened into opacity by laborious admixtures of language. This book is an attempt to make visible the invisible and distorting ruin, to cause it to cast a shadow. And because depression is the only life I have ever known, the thickened living you have in your hands is as discontinuous as the life—a mix of voices and tones, inconclusive, certainly unconcluded. It is in part what the doctors see and hear, write up, and call *depression*: the face darkened by grief, the whining and self-pity, the slump in the chair.

It is also a series of commentaries, and a scatter of entries from my diary. Some of these entries are sick with rage and the chant of self-extinction; some are so corroded by unreason that I cannot understand more than a few words here and there. But if these texts are here, firmly *kept* in this book at times against my better judgement, the point is not to disgust or confuse the reader, but to show, in the only way I know, the deranging hate we turn on ourselves constantly, secretly—a truth that would be lost to view in the clouds of smooth paraphrase or "objectivity."

For reasons I cannot explain, or perhaps for no reason at all, I have known that abysmal hatred, yet remained alive to write of it.

Others, many others, have not. Hence this book is not just "another life," but also something of a mystery, simply because I and it exist. To be chronically depressed and to tell of it is, in one sense, a contradiction.

Not that every instance of depression *must* end in death. Indeed, many have seen the dogs in the forest's half-light, been dragged to the very gate of the enemies' unambiguous lair, and lived. We may only be sure that our ruin and murder are what the dogs desire; after that, they desire to remain unseen, unbelieved in. If in writing this book I courted a certain disaster, this showing of the black dogs is done.

I do not wish to make the book seem reliable, or somehow *authoritative*. Freud observed about such a writer as I am:

"Shame before others is lacking in him, or at least there is little sign of it. One could almost say that the opposite trait of insistent talking about himself and pleasure in the consequent exposure of himself predominates in the melancholic."

The writing of this book has given such pleasure, which is the reason it should probably be viewed as suspect. The "insistent talking" Freud finds characteristic of neurotic behaviour has at the heart of it this churning silence, a will to concealment we cannot ever wholly extinguish, even when trying to write depression in its fullness and depth.

You have been warned.

CHAPTER 1

A Childhood in Light

In the beginning was summer and Spring Ridge, my father's cotton plantation in the South, and my room at dawn, its unlit fireplace and little yellow furniture brightened by first sunshine, sliced by slats of green shutters opening outward. Always, in the beginning: I am in the room in the house of angry silences at the edge of Spring Ridge's lands, deep in the north-Louisiana hills upcountry from the Red River.

Not far east of the house lay the ambiguous edge of the vast, damp bottomland, a first sinking of ground into the swamps and the low expanse of bayous, lazily winding between mud banks towards the river. When I was no older than four, hardly taller than a dog's front leg, I stalked crickets in the pasture near the house, picked blackberries in the bush alone, dredged for crayfish in the warm creek mud, anything to keep out of the angry house. Unless black mammy or white mother called, I followed strange sounds and tracks ever deeper down into the thickets and brambles.

The water moccasins—ugly, bad-tempered, jowls filled with poison, but too lazy to be *very* dangerous—awoke from their cold-minded naps at the sound of my scrambling, rolled off their logs into the day-dappled water, and twisted away across the warm bayou. I knew there were alligators there, somewhere, and longed to find one—monstrous and ancient, drowsing in the warm flood, horny snout and coldly glittering eyes just above the waterline. I never did.

In the beginning was the room on the south side of my father's angry house, and the first light of the summer dawn, then the truck, and my father, lifting me into the flat-bottom back, to ride with the help who lived too far away to walk in. We would go the rounds through early light in the truck—my father, his foreman and I—to pick up the field hands at their shacks deep in the pine bush, or at the end of narrow dirt roads disappearing into the woods, to the houses they lived in and we never saw, so deep in the pine and scrub they lay. I remember the lovely fragrance of smoke from pine-stoked cooking fires on their hard black arms, in the fabric of their clothes.

At noon, and at a honk from my father's truck, Big Joseph, huge and patriarchal as his name, whose sack I picked into when I chopped cotton in the morning, led me with a gentle black hand to the shady edge of the fields. He pissed heavy as a horse into the weeds, then we ate the lunches we had packed with us, while my father talked beside the truck with white men in khaki pants, khaki shirts, black leather belts. The meal finished, Big Joseph spread my napping blanket in the shady lee of field-edge bushes.

And of the nodding-off to afternoon slumber that came next, I remember these things: the glint of sunshine off the blackberries drooping in clusters from high mounds of tangled briars nearby; the nimbus of white-hot sun glowing around the dark silhouette standing over me; Big Joseph's soft voice, very distant in my memory now, telling me to come get him in the fields if I wanted anything; and my father's voice, yet more distant, and increasingly indistinct, speaking with the white men in khaki slacks and shirts very far away.

The air over the fields in late afternoon was stagnant, tired, dusty. Through that air, made gold by the wearying sun, the field hands came in from the cotton rows with their full sacks, gathering slowly towards my father and the truck, and I with them, small white hand in Big Joseph's huge black one.

In the house again, after dinner, with summer light vanishing behind dry trees, fireflies rising from the lawn under myrtle and magnolias, hate in the house coming up from the corners as darkness came when the daylight failed, I heard the voice of President Roosevelt in the dark brown parlour, the news of the war coming from the radio's arched dark-wood case.

I did not want to be in the room with the sullen silences that fell like heavy curtains between mother and father, parents and children. So I went elsewhere in the house, into Essie's hands, Mammy's hands, which scrubbed field dust and the day's sweat off my naked whiteness into the tub's turbid water.

---

7 November 1964

*Dry leaves clatter on the sidewalk, shattering under my
feet, under dry branches more nearly nude each day...
The first week of November and so little done, the clock
marching through the hours, and I have no time there—
I would break the faces of all the clocks and do away
with bells...*

*The leaves on the hills are bright flags announcing to
the sky that the earth will persevere, and we will
persevere in light. Flags of cloth rot are remembered by
the destroyers only as tattered symbols of other destroyers,
exploiters of the ground. But the flags of leaf will endure,
even in this destroying time, in the terror of turning
around to find myself always there, object of my desiring
and final annihilation. My intentions become impure.
And is this the inevitable magnetic north of my desire—
myself, steel point, hardened into one man bearing the
sins of the father towards the future generations?*

Of the light I loved as a child, none was more precious to me
than the evening radiance that gathered under the pecan tree and
in the rose gardens of my grandmother, deepening gradually
until the fireflies rose from the grasses and shrubs, winking on
and off in windward drifts across the lawns.

Here, on these fragrant grounds, around the ample, moth-
ering house painted palest rose-yellow and trimmed in white, in
the hilltop village of Greenwood—and never in my father's
house deeper down the country, at Spring Ridge—lay the emotional centre of what I was, and was to be.

The soft dusk lingered on the south verandah, a glow dim-
ming slowly behind large fig leaves planted close round the
porch. The buxom scent of smoke from the cigars of my grandfather and the planters and merchants of the neighbourhood lingered on the verandah's air, as the men smoked in their white
shirts and dark ties, talking with my father and grandfather
about the cotton, about politics, the war and weather. This was
my peace, among the men talking in the warm evening air
stirred into coolness by the verandah's ceiling fan.

While the slow talk drifted over me, I sat at the feet of these
men, playing with the toys my father had played with in that
house, his cast-steel painted train, his wooden alphabet blocks,

tiny bisque Mr. Penguin. And though I did not know the meaning of the letters on the blocks or in books, I looked at the coloured pictures in his huge floppy Buster Brown comic books in the failing light.

Or, becoming restless, I went inside, to the glazed-front bookshelves in the library, and pulled down one of the volumes that my grandparents, my father and Aunt Vandalia, his sister, had loved many years before. I remember the scent of aging Edwardian papers, the flower-children dancing in coloured lithographs, the fragility of pages, brittle, their edges gullied with tiny cracks from time and too much love.

At other times, while the men smoked cigars and the women drank lemonade in the parlour, I went into the hallway where the black Victrola stood, slid a heavy, hard disc from the stack inside the cabinet, cranked the spring, settled chin on knees tucked up under me on the staircase, and listened again and again to crackling recordings of the most beautiful voices in the world, made in the years before the other war, when my father was a boy.

It is in the house of that music, in rooms furnished with dark wooden chairs and tables and papered palest daffodil, among the fragrances of my grandmother's powders and old paper, the aroma of biscuits baked by my grandmother's cook—there, only there, in the aromatic memory of that vanished architecture is the falling, failing dusk in which I once wanted to live out all my days, and to which I still return in reverie.

I will take you there in language, make you believe so wonderful a place of light was real—and because you wish to believe, you will, and I will be satisfied by that fascination.

---

30 September 1965

*I would be a moth undistracted by candles, drawn only to
the central fire, to make the blaze brighter with my cinder.*

The shadow then will disappear, the death-shadow falling across the boy's path, his tattered remains. For again the Besetter sits at the door, harpies perch above the door, preening their black and oily wings—Again the stalking shadows of memory and fear are cast against the mind's wall. I believe God is the God of peace and of a sound mind—not of the lurking fears which come to me in the disastrous night....

Last night I lay on my back upon my narrow bed as God withdrew into nothing, and I heard the beating of calamitous wings, dispersing the seeds of me on the wind into rocky ground, into the moonless sky...I have heard the terrible flickering wings of disastrous angels, drowning sleep in the pale sheet-lightning of their nearness.

Today, now, writing in the hilltop cemetery of my people, the broken loom of bones on which my body was woven in darkness. My father, grandfather, uncles— buried flesh gone now, buried so many years ago, now ruins of bodies buried, quiet in the failing light of late afternoon—the sun, molten, dropping into night behind the trees, green so weary with the late summer heat, ready for first frost, months away.

I will never come here again, never again to lay violets on my father's grave...and the choir of crickets and locusts, gathering in the tired branches of the cemetery trees, a lethal tide of sound in the bushes—this knowing, theologizing, rational continent I am, being undone, worn slowly down, by the waves of that dry music...

I am very near the union of unestranged reality, the death I seek, seeking me—yet the reconciliation is not yet, and I cannot hear words that speak the time. All language stopped in cosmic aphasia.

———

Across this writing of my life, any telling of it to you, then falls
the darkness and the blood.

Always, first, the blood of a black man shot and dying, a field
hand of my father who had stumbled through the fields at night
to the house back at Spring Ridge, crawled onto the verandah
and collapsed in a damp heap. I watched the blood ooze from
under the dying man's body, pooling into a penumbra of red,
glowing around his body.

Then there was the blood of my father, soaking into the
summer-parched dirt of a country road in Oklahoma, where he
died, perhaps murdered, in August, 1947, and was left to be
found—or to be lost forever, as he was to me. I was not told he
was dead until weeks after my mother had received the news and
let him be put into the ground. In those weeks, a wall of
unspeaking and untelling arose around the ruined body, run over
by a circus man hurtling down the dark Oklahoma road, my
father's discoverer.

With my father gone, my mother sold his guns and farming
gear and took me away from Spring Ridge in the summer of my
seventh year. Shamed, abandoned by my father's family—blamed
unmercifully for driving him to death and drink because they
could not bear to blame him for bringing his disasters on himself—and with a young son to look after, Anne Bentley Mays
took refuge under the roof of her elder unmarried sister, my
Aunt Antoinette, in a nearby city.

It was then, I recall—upon moving from plantation to city,
country school to city school—that the bleeding darkness first
opened at the centre of myself. Until that time, even in the house
of anger, I had known where everyone stood, had learned the
hierarchy with language itself, and put my small hands into those
nearest me in the chain of Southern social being. Though not
yet seven, I knew my place in that chain exactly. Then suddenly
cast into the social sliding and mobilization of people in
America's postwar democracy, I could find no place to *be*.
Another boy, or sort of boy, caught in the same riptide of

change, might have found the break-out from plantation life liberating. I did not. I felt the very ground under my feet shaken, my roots ripped up, drying in the relentless sunshine of a new social day in America.

The blood comes into the story again, the pink blood of my mother this time, staining her pillows during the lung hemorrhages that came more frequently as cancer slowly killed her in the bedroom next to mine. And with the recollections of her dying come memories of the stench of cancerous rot, poisoning the air in the house. It lifted the day her gnawing disease killed her and she was taken away, five years after my father's vanishing and the final gathering of white cotton boles from those hot fields, the last ginning and binding into bales of cotton from that land.

I wept a little on the late spring afternoon my mother died, and then did not weep at all—felt nothing, in fact, neither sorrow nor grief. After that afternoon, I did not weep again in anyone's sight for many years, and never again at the death of anyone. In the strange logic being built in the emptiness where a boy had been, to weep would have been to acknowledge loss, hence love; and to love, to be loved—to be laid open to loss and grief—had already become horrifying to me. I observed but would not feel this leakage of existence, the unhealing wound within—or could not feel, since by that time I had almost certainly learned the tactics of self-annihilation, silent and invisible.

And why should I have not wanted to disappear forever? In the eyes of those left living and near after the death of my mother, I had ceased to be a boy and become a problem. For the aunt in whose house I lived, I was an unwanted burden, visited upon her by a widowed sister's premature death. For my dead mother's alcoholic father, forever obscenely sodden in another bedroom in my aunt's house, I was another gut needing food, when the only gut he wanted filled was his own. I had been a late child. My older sisters, gone and married, had rarely taken any interest in me; and now, with both parents dead, even that perfunctory interest vanished.

Cherished by no one, unwanted and unneeded by anyone, abandoned by father and mother, I devised a curious strategy that would harden into a frigid pattern before I was twelve. I would cherish nothing and no one, extinguish every desire to depend, need, want. I would abandon the body that had been abandoned by everyone else with firmness and finality. And because my body continued to exist, even though empty, I decided to fill it with the memory of my father, to become eternally the wonderful boy he was before he was ruined.

To fulfil this new, persistent longing—for death in the present and reincarnation in another body, my father's, and in another time—involved ceasing to exist. Yet because the body born in 1941, my body, continued to exist anyway, my every moment came to be tinted with a whining, insistent discontent.

Its inner agenda was, of course, self-slaughter. I had first learned its name and meaning not long after my removal to the city, when I stumbled upon a sob-sister magazine article about a little boy who killed himself by drowning. Reading that story was like receiving an answer to an unformed prayer; until then, I had not imagined that any deliberate way into forgetfulness existed.

The sweet, peaceable thought of self-administered death by water stayed with me for days, quieting my distress. At recess, I would go to the farthest corner of the school yard, and sit, imagining the slow slip into warm, still bayou water, imagine breathing the water deeply, my body sinking as my mind was painlessly overcome by sleep, extinction. It would be years before I learned that self-murder is not the sweet picture I imagined it to be on the playground, but violence, almost certainly pain, the infinitely wretched interval between the act and oblivion. It would be years before I recognized in this peaceful fantasia the final approach of the black dogs.

At the time, however, I was inclined to insist on the next dearest thing to self-annihilation: that I be allowed to leave my aunt's house in the city and go to the Edwardian house in the country, to live with grandmother and aunt and uncle in the house in which my father had been a boy. There the modern boy could be that other boy, his father, and be free at last of the unwanted body, the body unwanted by anyone.

For my mother's sister, such a move, however desirable it might have been from her standpoint, was unthinkable. She had vowed to my dying mother that I would be raised in the Church of Christ, Scientist, her sect and that of my mother, grandmother, great-grandmother, my sisters. For Aunt Antoinette, that commitment left any release of me out of the question. If, decades later, I would come to love her deeply, I despised her and her city house then, her religion's vague pieties, the stench of my grandfather's urine and wine, the school where I was shamed and bullied because I did not know the codes of boyhood in that fluid, postwar urban world.

The accidental discovery of masturbation was for me a sort of miracle, as helpful in its way as the thought of suicide: yet another mechanical way to strangle and annihilate the strong stirrings for intimacy without allowing intimacy itself. As I discovered, it was possible to reach orgasm quickly without sexual thoughts; to have sex without sexuality, without shame, or risk of admitting anyone into the silent secrecy I sheltered from the world. If masturbation, for most adolescents, is a first crucial step towards mature sexual imagination, for me it was a daily training in the extinction of erotic imaginations and fantasies, another kind of rehearsal for suicide, this time murder of the senses.

In those years, the dreams I allowed myself were never of sex, but of the bus trip to Greenwood, where Uncle Alvin waited at the bus station to drive me to Grandmother's, where dinner would be waiting in a dining room fragrant with oiled oak and old rouged silver. As the weather grew warm, dinner would be served at a table spread with white linen on the back verandah, beyond which lay broad pastures, fragrant with new-cut hay or mock orange blossoms, and the perfumes of old roses blooming in the back garden.

Saturdays I would spend alone, being the boy I believed my father to have been—curled up with his Woodcraft Indians books in an old leather chair in front of the bedroom fireplace, or hiking through the swamps deep in woods beyond the cemetery and collecting empty birds' nests, or drawing up plans for the tiny airplane I would someday build, like the workable one he had bought in kit form, assembled and buzzed over the town in when he was a lad of sixteen. Sunday mornings would be spent in the little, elegant church of my grandmother; then at noon we gathered around the ample table, eating chicken fried perfectly by the black cook. Sunday afternoons would be darkened by an ever-deepening dread of the obligatory trip back to the city, to the house stinking with my grandfather's wine and urine, to the school where I was ridiculed for the strange tales I told of a boyhood, mine and not mine, that had passed fifty years before.

At last, in the summer of my fifteenth year, there came a Sunday afternoon when the dread was too strong for me to overcome. The rising acid of hatred in my throat, the stinging nostalgia for the lost paradise I imagined I had found in my grandmother's house, all finally combined into a decision not to go back to the city. So I stayed; and, to the distress of Aunt Antoinette, I never went back. That autumn, I enrolled in the school from which my father had graduated, valedictorian, wreathed in honour, beloved—at least in the tales told of him, and in my obsession-ridden dream of his life, now mine.

---

16 July 1966

*My father was born on this mid-summer day, who is
now a myth to me. I cannot remember his voice—I try,
but cannot remember. Nights of tears come back to me,*

*shed into my pillow for years after his death, days come
back to me when I sat in the cemetery by his grave,
hearing only the silence, and nothing of the birds or the
whispers of wind in dry branches...the only syllables
breaking the silence: two white sounds, the gravestones
of grandfather and father...*

*How could you come here, father, in this university
hall so far from all you were? How could you bear to see
your son, your first-born and only son, naked and
worthless in this future of which you knew nothing?*

*I would embrace you, if you would have me, lie naked
on your chest and listen to your beloved heart unbeating
now, shield you from the rage of stars, and years and the
hatreds that have laid waste my soul, too....*

*Then at last the love of you would wash the memories
away, and then my flowing blood would wash my mind
and all the bitter memories away, and wash your body
clean. I would listen to the life in you that is my life,
then go with you into the unliving and the silence, to
lie beside you unto the ages of ages unknowing...*

In the August I defected to the country, I spent much time
thinking about the school I would be attending come fall. In the
last hot days of summer fantasy, I imagined that I would walk
from the garish polychrome culture of the 1950s into a sepia-
toned photograph where I would again have a place within the
old, stable village order still alive in my grandmother's mind, in
her house, among her acquaintances.

Though I had left the city and moved in among the toys and
books, fetishes of my father's childhood, I could not stop the
progress of the clock's thin, inexorable hands. When I arrived for
the first day of classes overdressed, I recall, or perhaps merely
dressed in a faintly old-fashioned way, I stepped into a society of
boys with duck-tails and girls with bubble hairdos hardened with

plastic spray, of basketball players, fans of Frank Sinatra and Elvis Presley—a society almost exactly like the one I had left behind in the city high school, except in rural miniature.

Still, I was comforted to find that the "good" boys and girls, the children of my father's peers with whom I had occasionally played on the weekend trips to Greenwood, were in ascendancy at the school. They were the ones who picked from their own number the recipients of honours or offices, who tacitly set the rules of costume and behaviour, who regulated the passage from outside to inside the school élite. My transit into the privileged circle was assured—or so I believed.

As surely as I had been cloistering myself for years in a dark, ramshackle retreat cobbled from old photographs, half-remembered tales about my father and props and books, memories from childhood awash in light, my privileged high-school peers had found their places in the swiftly transmuting American culture around 1960. In my sepia-toned photographic tableau, the village blacks were still servants, and the white élite were masters; in the real world, racial segregation was under attack. My peers, by and large, would accept this change; at the time, I could not tolerate it.

Another problem for me—a mutation much more threatening, since it even more drastically undermined the codes of hierarchy—was the quiet, gradual abandonment of the ethic that had always prevailed among rural Southern adolescents of my crowd, from well before my father's generation. This code had ordained perpetual premarital virginity for girls, out-of-town whoring and drunkenness for boys, scorn and ostracism for young women who "fell," shotgun weddings and banishment for unmarried social equals who found themselves expecting, and, for the rest, eventual settlement into lifelong marriages that would weld both partners permanently into the steel grid of village elderhood. It hardly needs to be said that this "code" was always more fiction than fact, though occasionally useful as a solemn pretext for arbitrary punishments and rewards.

The traditional white matriarchy to which my grandmother and Aunt Vandalia belonged was aware that change was underway. There was abroad in the land a certain new, disquieting casualness about sex and divorce, a relaxed social style requiring none of the propriety and exquisitely tuned hypocrisy necessary for the conduct of life in strictly coded cultures. They complained about it, but to no avail: my peers had lost interest in perpetuating the structures and strictures, moral elegances and techniques of power required to maintain control of the village that, in any case, was becoming the domain of other, new people. None of my intelligent, ambitious friends had any intention of remaining in Greenwood; nor would any of them, after university, return. Thus, the elderhood itself was doomed. In my last years of high school, my last years in Greenwood, I found myself torn between my hunger to belong among my peers and their parents, to please them by doing the new things they did, and inward, quiet horror at their sexual, social, intellectual *Americanization.*

Upon graduating from high school, the ruling high-school clique gave me the award generally reserved for a conspicuous oddity in its midst: *Graduate Most Likely To Succeed.*

----

9 December 1966

*I recollect the violent thunderstorms that came from the
south-west on afternoons when I was small, chasing me
into the house from the woods and from my secret places
in the yard,*
   *I recollect the sunsets after, golden stalks and sprays
of light springing from behind black clouds passing
westward, towards Texas...I remember the shaded edge
of the plantation, gift of father to son, wedding-gift of
grandfather to my father, both dead, buried and now
bones in the hill my people bury on—and the South,
and the past that is the South*

*—I am so weary now, so weary of the nowness of
it—but the places in the South, in the past,
are mine, springs to go back to when my throat is
dry. These, I can remember when everything else is
nothing, or until I have no mind to remember, until
I have gone into the utter unbeing my father ever
tended towards, and I tend to with him, and with all
the living—*

———

Eight years passed between the time I left Greenwood School and the critical summer of 1967, when I worked and became ill in Ireland—indistinct, unmemorable years of Southern undergraduate university education and Northern graduate work in old-fashioned English studies, philology and bibliography and such. All of it was a slow drift on rafts of scholarships and honours towards, I imagined vaguely if at all, a doctorate in literature. I had no friends; the agenda, becoming ever more clear, was eventual disappearance into a place where friends would be unnecessary.

However twisted it would have seemed to others, had I made it wholly public, the first shape of this vanishing still bore a recognizable human countenance. The project was a gradual detachment from the democratic, liberal and secularized culture into which I had been displaced after my father's death, and the establishment of a little duchy of the spirit, autocratic and chaste. Mine was an eccentricity typical of Americans, ranging in its expressions from the foolish *faux*-medievalizing of tycoons like Citizen Kane to the transatlantic fugues and anti-democratic *hauteur* of T. S. Eliot and Ezra Pound. My advanced academic work in early English was a step towards a similar end: first the doctorate, then the job in a small, élite Southern college, where I could at last disappear into literature and obscurity, an imaginary feudal past, anti-American, and above all anti-modern.

I cannot say exactly when this will to vanish began to sharpen and darken into something else, a menace stalking my steps, infesting my dreams. But the haunting fear that I would never be able to realize the plan, *that the body I was born with would never disappear*, dawned with special force after my arrival for advanced graduate study in that state of mind I called "the North."

There, in the homeland of that threatening horde of *Americans*, I first encountered, at close range, young men and women, people wholly outside the hierarchical universe given me by my grandparents' house—the universe of servants and masters, social equals and superiors and inferiors, each human order inscribed with codes binding all orders into coherence. Outside the university, I believed, lay nothing but the chaos and drift of a modern, suburbanizing world. I decided to finish graduate work as quickly as possible, then leave the North forever. But as I worked towards the advanced degrees that would earn me passage back to the South, I clung all the more fiercely to the moral tapestries and social etiquette of the Edwardian Southern childhood I never had, to an antiquated aristocratic bearing stitched together from legends, family habits, and an inner absence of feeling that in every way resembles, but is not, snobbery.

For example, an invitation to dinner at the home of fellow students, a couple from New York City, had to be declined because the couple was not married; I could not imagine sitting at table with a man and woman, unmarried yet openly living together. From the moment we met in the North, I was much drawn to a brilliant Southern classmate, a convert from esoteric mathematics to English medieval studies—until I discovered that his rural family were what my people would call "uncultivated," a polite way to say *white trash*—whereafter the relationship became impossible. The antique social code in which I was attempting to keep myself corseted decreed that white trash are always untrustworthy, devious, deceitful, especially when made shiny by a patina of advanced education. Such self-constructed

unreality in which I moved and existed was all beginning to be
less and less manageable; leaks and cracks began to appear. *I
accomplish nothing because I am nothing, the ground and cause of
innumerable mistakes*, reads an entry written in my diary when I
was twenty-five. *I am become the bleakness of lists and schedules, a
mechanical going. When I hate, it will be coldly. There must be no
sudden moves in this slip back, nothing to attract attention—only
recession into failing light, then night, then nothing.*

*Dim, untrussed and undone night, in the cellar of myself, vermin
rustle among the pages of undone work...These pages dirtied with
contradictions, journals of days shapeless, falling—sprawling records
of attempts, failures, more failures. But each time the busy mind
finds in itself the flaw, I must rip the stencil off to get at facts, only to
find patternless constellations, infinities of nothing. Even echoes of
the voice of God my Lord become impossible to make out, in the
dark under shadowy brambles beyond the edges of the cotton patch,
margins of bright field. I am become so old there, so very old.*

———————

I did not realize at the time how energetically I was con-
structing—at the expense of virtually every other project of the
will—an imaginary body, utterly subject to me sensuously and
intellectually, a mechanism workable in the world from within
my darkness. I hated the worthless body I was born with; it
seemed to be continually *demanding, urging*. When I satisfied it
by masturbating, I did so without pleasure or fantasy, quickly,
only to get release from nagging chthonic urges. It never
occurred to me to buy an erotic magazine, to read an erotic
story; I had no sexual imagination, nor did I want one.

The imaginary body I was building, on the other hand,
demanded nothing, and served me in almost everything. If I had
successfully completed it, this body would have enabled me to
play out a petrified, antiquated humanism, which I was determined to produce, stage, star in, die in, surrounded by the tattered props of a lost world of gentility, dignity, authority.

I recall an autumn afternoon, while preparing for an American literature seminar, when I heard my own soul's clock ticking in the dark first pages of Herman Melville's *Moby Dick*— "whenever I find myself growing grim about the mouth; whenever it is a damp, drizzly November in my soul; whenever I find myself involuntarily pausing before coffin warehouses, and bringing up the rear of every funeral I meet…"

As the black dogs tighten their circle, they often bring with them the certainty Ishmael mused of, as he hauled his carpet-bag through foggy, night-bound streets in a bid to escape from the world's unbearable weariness. "Yes, these eyes are windows, and this body of mine is the house. What a pity they didn't stop up the chinks and the crannies though, and thrust in a little lint here and there. But it's too late to make any improvements now. The universe is finished; the copestone is on, and the chips were carted off a million years ago."

Like other contemporary melancholics, and unlike Ishmael, my Romantic predecessor, I have never felt the urge to visit coffin factories and attend to funeral rites for the unknown. We feel no need to seek out gloomy settings appropriate to the sickening self-pity that comes with depression's onset, since we ourselves have become such sites. We are both the coffins, in which the children we once were are laid out, and the corpses. We are, at once, cortege and grave-digger, mourners and priest, dying again and again, being lowered into a pauper's grave, in the living death of our disorder. Ours are the hands that take up the pen after the funeral and write in the parish register the bald notice of yet another death, another victory for the unmeaning that the depressed believe haunts the world.

———

The ramshackle, melancholy body that lived for me in the world, had I completed building it, would have been a wonder of priggishness and fastidious attention to decorum and dress, of ostentatious romanticism and abstemious avoidance of romance. This body would have also been punctilious in its religious fidelity and high, autocratic piety—the only qualities I did not inherit more or less naturally from my family, and that therefore had to be constructed from almost nothing. The construction began when I was a teenager, as a slow, strong move into the Episcopal Church, and culminated with my reception into that church in the autumn of 1966.

The attraction lay in Anglicanism's venerable intellectual and literary tradition, with which graduate studies in English had richly acquainted me. Even though disestablished at the time of Revolution in America, the tiny Episcopal Church was a shrine in which broad, humane learning was honoured, liberal piety was expected, splendid and antiquated ceremonies were performed without embarrassment and all of it in precincts heavy with the scent of old, established social power and respectability.

However warped the motives behind it, my conversion was without cynicism or opportunism. At an early age, during my first encounters with confident atheists and pagans in university, I found myself dismayed by their comfortable self-congratulation, the smug simplicity of imagining that an idea of such immense antiquity, force and endurance in Western culture as theism, and its historic forms and rites, could be merely *ignored.* I did not, and do not, believe it can be.

And, in any case, a simple Episcopal service of Morning Prayer I attended when still a teenager had captured my shrinking heart and imagination. For years after that service, I attended Episcopal churches wherever I lived, reading its history and theology and spirituality, studying its relation to the ancient and pre-Reformation churches. Though I would not have put the case this way then, I had discovered in Anglicanism the splendid, antique mantle with which to clothe the naked body I had constructed from dust, photos, memories, the histories and affectations of others. Whatever other grace it bestowed, the solemn laying-on of the Bishop's hands confirmed the imaginary distance I sought to put between myself and American religious fundamentalism, populism and vulgar anti-Communism, and the modern mass democracy I loathed.

––––––––––

Because they had seen it coming, my Christian Scientist relatives were quiet in their disapproval. They had concluded when I left the city for Greenwood that I would not adopt the faith of Mrs. Eddy. My Confirmation appalled my Methodist kin.

I was not moved by this response, since my decision was, in large part, an act of resistance to a failure and treason they had come to represent for me. Sturdy Methodists of the South for generations, my father's people had felt deep loyalty to their respectable and respected evangelical church, publicly supporting its traditional liberalism, ecumenism and social conscience through the Jazz Age, Depression and the years of world war.

But whatever tolerance and cosmopolitan charity these relatives shared with members of other U.S. denominations considered "respectable"—Presbyterian and Episcopalian, principally— were swept into shambles by the McCarthyism, conspiracy fantasies and anti-Communist paranoia that tided across North America in the 1950s. My Methodist relatives, or at least the most energetically pious among them, responded first with indifference, then with what I considered vulgar enthusiasm, before eventually falling away into a brittle simulation of their prim Methodist lives before the coming of malls, the trailer parks, the anti-Communist televangelists.

I would not be mentioning this surge of narrow-minded, populist sensibility, so foreign to the Southern élite's adulation of the quintessential Episcopalian nob Franklin D. Roosevelt, had it not been the ideological cutting edge of a profound social change I felt and despised. And because I despised the change, I despised my Methodist family for their complicity in it.

A long-ignored stratum of white American society, middle-class and "new"—Irish and Italian and other immigrants of the late-nineteenth century, that is—was hurling its postwar wealth and youth against the timbers of old élite restraint in the name of anti-Communism, snubbing the polite disdain with which my family had kept the "others" in abeyance, and dropping even token respect for the code, rule and tradition which my family had used to protect its privileges for generations. My fictive self would resist all that, and distance itself from what I believed to be my family's failure to resist to the death the mass society that took shape in America in the wake of the Depression and war.

------

3 April 1967

*Then there was God, then the laying on of hands and
then there was not God—a silence in the room—after
the words of rite had dissolved into the silence—
nothing—I had married books, the Bible, the Prayer
Book but not the Body of Christ—a disappearance in
the room, as God disappeared into books, gleaming brass
fittings, the lingering odors of incense under pitched oak
roof after the Holy Eucharist, and the emptying of the
Church—What did I do in that November sinking
by the altar rail, under episcopal hands and the Holy
Spirit, into nothing?*

The elaborate tomb I had systematically, energetically built did not come crashing down all at once. Throughout my life, at least since adolescence, intermittent tremors had been shaking loose bits of masonry, requiring new outlays of energy and attention to keep this unhappy architecture intact.

Towards the end of 1966 and the completion of course-work for a master's degree, the effort required by these rehearsals had become extreme, exhausting, virtually all-consuming. It was in those final weeks that I began attending to a fellow graduate student, a man about twenty-five, my age at the time. I did not recognize my interest for the lust it was, at least not at first. I had no experience of sex, or disciplining lust into strategy, directed towards fulfilment. So I watched, powerless to do anything else. In this episode, I assiduously hid my feelings from myself even as they led me obsessively back to the places where I could see this man—all the while hiding (or so I thought) these compulsions from him.

Then came the late afternoon in December, 1966, that I saw what I was in the face of another. The blunt confrontation was with a third man, the graduate student's roommate—his lover, I suspected, though perhaps I only imagined that because of the strident jealousy driving his words to me. His accusation, as I recall, had to do with the cowardice of my uncarefully hidden homoerotic gazing, warnings against interloping, poaching. It was the first time I had been exposed, or seen myself, as desiring, incomplete—the first time the reality of craving an existence outside the inexorable bonds of my inner contract of chastity had been driven into the open.

From that moment of intense pain and embarrassment, and over the next eighteen months, whatever mental and physical well-being I had previously enjoyed began to deteriorate rapidly. I left graduate school at the end of term, and spent the next several months in the Louisiana house of my grandmother, doing very little on my academic project—the critical edition of a Middle Scots poem, my masters thesis—and churning restlessly inside a closed, dark drum of mixed feelings, anxieties, sometimes terrors, all provoked by an increasing inability to keep erotic desire damped down, extinguished.

I could be that antique person only in the loneliness of my book-lined rooms. The thought that outside my study people were meeting, friendships were being made, sex initiated and risked in nakedness and enjoyed came to me as afflictions, since I believed that such encounters were forbidden to me. To be sure, the fabric of fantasy was by that time becoming almost unbearably heavy, and beginning to unravel at the same time, leaving

me burdened in mental clothes old, dark and frayed. I described
my bitter childhood to those willing to hear, and declared my
determination to crusade against the disarray visited upon the
world by everything modern, but mostly I complained.

---

12 April 1967

Nothing—the worthlessness of the gazing, hateful
watching his body in the university library, watching
for it—He sat at another table, would get up from his
etymological encyclopedias, and stand for an instant,
desirable in the man he was, that I am not—young as I
am old, moving with no shame as I walked with shame
in that desiring, him, depleted by the hateful gazing—

It was while complaining that I discovered a curious fact: that
even as my work of desperate psychic repair became increasingly
exclusive, jeopardizing even my studies, so was I becoming an
increasingly exotic object of interest to other students.

In that interest, I found a temporary ease. For the wealthy,
Ivy-League educated young of Westchester County, for sleekly
secularized urban moderns reared in New York City or
Philadelphia or Boston—men and women my age in earthly
years but from some vastly younger planet of imagination—a
creature, a Southerner of my sort, was an extraordinary curiosity.
What appealed, I found, was the way my tales always began with
the fairy-tale sense, if not the actual locution, of "once upon a
time...," once upon a memory, once upon an old photograph,
recollecting a Southern plantation childhood only half-lived, and
half-fashioned from memories handed down by grandparents,
servants, relatives.

It was an interest I exploited. In unrolling the carpet of
curious narratives for complicit spectators, and in those observers'

willing belief in the images inscribed in the warp and weft of the cloth, the breaking, fading threads were temporarily twisted back together, the oppressive wholeness restored. In these performances, there was of course no question of intimacy or vulnerable friendship, since I was not then, had never been, capable of sustaining either.

What emerged, in the place of intimacy, was a strange personal metaphorics. As I told my stories I began to explain to myself that my unhappiness was not mine, but that of the frightened boy I must protect, the frightened Edwardian child who must not grow up, my father.

To that end, I had to keep him within me, clean, civilized, pure, and noble forever. Now, as always, I was nothing, no one except the guardian of the dead Edwardian boy, who had become a man, a calamity, incidentally the engenderer of the son I am. He was the victim of time, of growing up, against which I must protect him. The contract I had made with myself, before adolescence, was that I must become a living sacrifice, a scapegoat wandering in desolation, for the sins of my father. My atonement would only be fulfilled by the emptying of my life of any existence separate from his, by remaining the Edwardian boy he had been before being ruined—a stance that would eventually require the shedding of my blood. Hence, the melancholy desire for death, my constant meditation; hence, too, the ease with which mental rehearsals of self-slaughter have always come to me.

In fact, I knew, and know, very little about the Edwardian boy, my father, and little about the man, other than his absence. There exists in my mind only the picture of a tall, slender, handsome man about forty, dressed in khaki shirt and slacks and wearing (as was then the custom among the sons of planters in the South) a khaki-coloured pith helmet. I know this son of a wealthy cotton planter and merchant did exist, that he was an alcoholic and womanizer who liked flying his airplanes and hunting with the menfolk of the family in faraway places, and who despised the settled routines imposed by home life and parenthood and the

cotton crop. Years before he abandoned the world altogether—so
I deduce from rare comments made by my sisters, the odd scrap
of evidence overheard, or discovered in one of the innumerable
scrapbooks and notebooks and diaries kept by Aunt Vandalia
and my grandmother—my father had abandoned his wife sexu-
ally, and his daughters and son emotionally. Perhaps he had
never had any feelings for them at all, and was happy only with
his father, cousins and male buddies, drinking and driving fast,
or hunting big game in Mexico or the Baja.

Only one sequence of mental images remains with me, from
one night and the following day: a cheap motel room with lami-
nated wood furnishings; a man, my father, and a woman I did
not know; a glass of orange juice beside my bed; the face of my
mother, crying in bitterness and rage, after we got home the next
morning to find that my maternal grandmother had died during
the night of my father's absence.

His absence from home, his absence for me from birth to the
time of his passing out of existence forever—these and other
absences sometimes made me wonder whether he was ever present in the world at all—or merely a shadow in a few photographs, an incubus who came to my mother at night,
impregnating her with the seed of me, then vanishing into the
mist of unknowing that falls now between him and me.

In the years I carried the dead boy on my back, trying to keep
him from quickening into manhood, I knew almost nothing
about the historical person he grew up to be. Following his final
withdrawal, the announcement of his death, and our move from
plantation to city, my mother never spoke of him; nor did my
Aunt Antoinette. His sister, Aunt Vandalia, and his mother
would only tell me that he was someone everyone loved and no
one feared—that he was innocent of anything I might hear said
against him, that he was a victim of malice, perfectly blameless.

There is nothing in any of this to account for the self-
negating I imposed on myself in his name—the retroactive
redemption, the strange unrequited love I had felt for him since

his disappearance. Yet the vow I enjoined on myself, in some moment buried too deeply in the mind to rediscover, was to remain pure, a virgin in every sense; a body dead in all ways— devoid of emotion, longing, regret—except for those certain animal and mental movements necessary to carry on the role. To find that I was something else than he was would be to lose him utterly, to fail to keep him alive in the mind as the highly promising, intelligent boy he had been, and thus protect him from growing up into disgrace. He never told me he loved me.

───────────

At first the vow and the life I crafted to fulfil it were all fiction, a role I could play while still knowing the difference between it and another life. But gradually, with a kind of remorseless force, this fiction began to be more desirable than any other life I could imagine. At last, I had become an ongoing spectacle of abjection, unable to take off the mask and costume of ruin.

It never occurred to me that, even if they were intrigued at first, my listeners would eventually find their roles as spectators of my mounting self-abnegation offensive. Nor did I understand that playing the role of witness to outpourings of confessional melancholy is nobody's idea of good friendship. Or that count- less people with hard-luck childhood stories go ahead to lead productive and happy adult lives, and there was no ostensible reason why I should not become one of them.

I was certainly not prepared to admit that, increasingly, my "personal" transactions with other people tended to be set-ups by both parties—a passing amusement on their part, a confir- mation of worthlessness and undesirability on mine. Looking back at this history, I find it unsurprising that I have no friend- ships that took firm root until after the catastrophic breakdown in my twenty-eighth year, the event that would begin to set me, if not free, then a little more free than I had been.

Had the soulful confidence games I played with my intelligent colleagues in graduate school been intended to get something tangible or desirable—money, sex, power, even a little human intimacy—they might have been rather sleazy, or perhaps pathetic as well as sleazy, but not sick. Two things, both of which I only dimly recognized, made them sick.

The first was the fact that they were calculated to avoid fulfilment of the common human needs of intimacy, sex and power. Sensible, desirable people do not necessarily flee close contact with people made depressed and anxious by this materialistic, greedy world. They will flee, however, when the histrionics exceed ordinary revulsion at the shadow Enlightenment has cast over the world. They will do so when the play becomes an empty panegyric to a fictive time when honour and civic decency counted for all, the mere accumulation of money for nothing.

And so they should flee from me, I told myself with relief and in the self-dramatizing way characteristic of people drunk on self-serving fantasy. Otherwise, I would run the risk of becoming involved in the machinations of the greedy, demotic world. I must remain pure, keep the boy inside me untouched by base human emotions, uninvolved in the coarse doings of ordinary young people, continuously rejected. Hidden behind the manifest narratives of woe was that secret vow—secret from everyone, even myself, that is, until a young doctor named David helped me unmask it.

The second thing that made these tactics sick is that I was becoming increasingly aware of their sickness, while remaining loyal to them with more ferocity than ever. Hence, my self-loathing and indecency—traits confirmed in my mind when the healthy auditors and spectators of this play of self-pity gradually realized their complicity in my narcissistic exploitation and turned away.

———

16 April 1967

tonight a song I have heard before comes to me, I have

received it before in the freight the wind of memory
carries....a guitar's song, knowing and telling of the old
people and the old ways swept into time's darkness—the
dying of the time, the South and of the light, all dying
in your grave, father, cut deep in the hill of our people—
the first American John Mays, born 1615 in Virginia,
Matthew Mays born 1730 in Virginia who died young,
leaving John Mays to go with his remarried mother
Dorcas Abney to South Carolina, and there are others
coming from these loins: John Mays, great-grandfather
born in South Carolina, witness to the horror of Civil
War, perpetrator of it, dying 1923, wealthy in east
Texas—John Mays my grandfather, John Mays—you,
my father, with them all, decomposing into your grave,
dying in memory, in graves cut into the red-dirt hill of
our people, out of town, far from the destroyers now—

You all turned away at last.

You withdrew, one by one, into whatever light you believed
to be life, away from the pseudo-life I had built, the peculiar,
twilit architecture of ceaseless self-pity. By the time I left the university at Christmas, 1966, my old soulful stories, draped in
Spanish moss and scented with the decadent odour of wilting
magnolia blossoms, had become repulsive to me, and so unbearable to you that I finally gave up the telling.

CHAPTER 2

Nightfall

In the fall of 1966, as you were all turning away, I got wind of a job opportunity that would have appealed to any normally pedantic student in my field of English studies. It held a peculiar attraction for me.

The work involved the preliminary survey and cataloguing of an odd assortment of books that had been discovered a few years earlier in a cathedral town on the central Irish plain. It appears that two, perhaps more, eighteenth-century bishops in the Church of Ireland—as the tiny handful of Anglicans on the Catholic island have called themselves since the Reformation—

were ardent bibliophiles and humanist scholars, learned gen-
tlemen of the sort British bishops, until recently, often were.
Over the decades, they had amassed a huge diocesan library, and
lodged it in the upper storey of an unused stone building on the
cathedral grounds, where it was gradually forgotten by subsequent bishops, deans and layfolk.

Until, that is, a new and intellectually curious dean arrived at
the cathedral in the early 1960s. After settling in to his new job,
he asked the sexton for a key to the forgotten building at the
graveyard's edge, and there found the cold, mouldering library.
Among the first books he opened was a tome in modern binding,
brought off the press in the fifteenth century—a priceless volume
from the earliest moments of printing. Then he found a first edition of *The Faerie Queene*, and another of Newton's *Principia*.
The dean kept opening, looking—gradually realizing that he had
by chance become the keeper of one of Ireland's great treasures, a
library that embraced all the humanistic and scientific learning
of its era in books of high rarity and beauty.

He needed a bibliographer, and let it be known to anyone he
thought might be able to find him one. I heard of the job from an
elderly university librarian, a convert to Roman Catholicism who
had recently visited the derelict quarters of the collection while on
a sort of pious Grand Tour of the world's Catholic countries.

I wrote to the dean, explaining my qualifications—intense
coursework in the exacting history of printed books—and got
the job. By late spring, 1967, when I left the little Southern town
of Greenwood *en route* to Ireland in order to start the long, lonesome four months of sorting the library, I believed I had at last
found a way into "another life," as Kristeva called the uncompli-
cated universe of depression—a life apart from the modernity
that frightened me, the tempting complicities that froze my soul
into absurd postures, shutting me into a house apart from the
complicated lives of people around me, and which I loathed.

I imagined the part I was to learn in Ireland was that of
pedant and fusty scholar, moving slowly and alone among the

books. It was to be a play in the shadow-land of the real world from which I was estranged, a shuffling through a moonscape waste and dry. I already dressed the part: oddly for my age, too formally. I walked unsmiling on city streets, with eyes always downcast towards pavement or earth. The body that had walked since I was a boy would at last become almost a zero, immediately communicating to the world outside that it wanted nothing, no acknowledgement or feeling, and did not want to acknowledge or feel or otherwise be disturbed. The only remaining problem for the zero was that it *had* to be in a body: either one given at birth or, like mine, one constructed.

A library in Ireland, a room into which none could come but me, was what my tiny zero mind wanted, a place where I could speak the language of self-hatred and of self-pity and encounter no resistance. If depression is indeed another life, lived with grudging willingness in grief's shadow and haunted by echoing voices from the past and realm of the dead, it is also a life of cowardice, induced because depression forbids a more risky, daring life. At last, the tiny zero wishes to be alone in its infinite boredom and weariness. As I dozed across the Atlantic towards Ireland, I already had in mind a cold, high room of books surrounded by the green of a cathedral close, a room devoid of all the people who had turned away, and to whom, in any case, I had become sick to death of talking.

---

1 May 1967

—writing scratchy from trembling hand, made to quake
by engines lifting hand and body from ground, Kennedy
left behind under the Aer Lingus plane, taking it all,
hand and body, towards Newfound-land, by the
southern tip of Green-land, finally to Ire-land, all
lands of nothing I know of—
...later—a brittle star, cold, frozen still blank dark

sky out the window
*   ...later—recollecting Greenwood, the months home*
after Indiana, in my room again—and the photographs
I found in the attic boxes, of them, the ancestors, to sift
through until my hands were dusty with fine rot and
decaying emulsion—it was that, and the unfeeling that
came with looking at them, unfeeling about God,
nothing there, not even the absence of God I have lived
in, not even that—only dust on my fingers of sepia
chemicals, in my nostrils, slowly eroded by time's scrape
and weather from the old paper of photographs—

On the early May morning I arrived in Ireland, the dean of the
cathedral whose library I was to catalogue drove me in his little
car through a radiantly green landscape made almost unspeakably beautiful by the brilliant golden cascades of gorse blooms
and the intense blue sky. The scattering of white on the higher
hills was a snowfall from the night before, not yet melted.

After lunch at the deanery, we visited the library, on the upper
storey under its raftered roof. If mentally exhausted from antici-
pation and months of struggling against darkness, and physically
tired from the transatlantic flight, I was nevertheless pierced by
an acute sense of home-coming. I had found the room I had
been searching for.

The oak shelving in the gloomy attic was stacked high with
thousands of leather-bound books, touching virtually every subject of human interest: poetry and biblical commentary, natural
history and medicine, geography and physics, politics and architecture. The dark brown panorama of books spoke to me of
solemn learning, but also of recession and decline. For even as
the bishops had been compiling this splendid collection, the
Anglican presence in Ireland was dwindling from a vital religious
practice into an hereditary aristocratic taste, the perfunctory faith
of an increasingly tiny minority. And with that decline in

church-going came the fading of any memory that, in the dank attic, lay a library of wonders.

It was forgotten, as I wished to be forgotten. It had been allowed to lapse into dereliction, as I wanted my body to lapse into decay. My intention was not to be rediscovered.

The prying imagination of the dean, whose cathedral congregation of a dozen or so souls left him with little to do other than poke about the neighbourhood, had found all manner of archaeological remnants and historical curiosities to keep busy his otherwise bored spirit. He burned with the genteel, eccentric antiquarianism that often displaces love in bright clergy who have lost faith in divinity and humanity. But my stay would not be long enough to allow him to discover my secrets. Living under the roof of his eighteenth-century deanery, working in his library, I could be a book, unopened for centuries, dead to prying minds.

From the day I arrived in Ireland, my dwindling reserves of energy were spent toiling, or appearing to toil, on the bibliographical listing of the works. But much of my diminishing will was squandered fighting the library's mixed fascination and suffocation. The suction of the chilly, damp attic frightened me. I could not escape the sense that I was leaking into the books, my existence was turning into text, forgotten on closed vellum pages; whatever I had been was being displaced by words.

Yet wasn't it precisely *this*—I asked myself in the diary entries, as the distress deepened—that I had most keenly wanted? Was it not this very discipline of disappearance, leakage into unbeing? Whence, then, the continual dread?

---

26 May 1967

in the library alone
  cold and damp air all musty and still within, a steady
rain falling on the eaves, on the intensely green cathedral
close...

pulling down book after book from the shelves,
unopened for centuries, writing an entry for it in tiny
hand on a rectangular reference card—catchwords and
foliations, colophon and collation, folio/octavo/quarto,
etc., edition, impression—Ronald B. McKerrow, An
Introduction to Bibliography for Literary Students
(Oxford: Oxford University Press, latest impression
[1962]); heilige Schrift of us, puddling into pedantry—
today: discovered a dust-smothered first edition of
Paradise Lost, first editions of Boyle, Locke, incunabula,
all left so many summers ago to sleep on shelves, left
upwards of two centuries ago for me to wake them up
today...

there, in masonry and cold plaster, the library wall
between me and all beautiful things, forbidding my
participation, keeping chastity I want to keep, do not
want to keep—while I believe that one thing only can
release me, melt the glass wall, release me into the
unchaste world—a consuming love of the vanquished
God...

I had been in the nearly complete isolation of rural Ireland for just a few weeks, when the everyday rains, ordinarily pleasant and brief, began to come more frequently. As summer came on, the rains showed no signs of letting up. First thought fugitive, a mere aberration destined not to last long, the steady downpours began to blight the ordinarily bright weathers of an Irish summer. When they settled in at last, refusing to go away, the constant showering became a topic of much conversation, and finally, after widespread flooding, of national public concern.

The damp and cold that came with the endless rain at first induced a pleasing, sensual melancholy in me. As the downpours continued, I seemed to become one with the soaked ground of the green cathedral close, its soil brittle with bones from burials over centuries, my soul as damp and grey as the church's rain-darkened stone cladding. The bibliographical work before me seemed to blur and smear, as though the volumes were dissolving, the printing leached away by the never-ending rain, making it impossible for me to read the titles properly.

And like the ground, the books, the buildings, I, too, began to leak physically. To my mind's eye, cluttered with words and literary conceits by then, I had begun to turn into a ribald Renaissance allegory of the Irish weather—or so the intestinal infection appeared to me at the time, when I thought the general dissolution of worlds was exactly what I wanted.

The disorder began with knife-like cramps. It quickly developed into miserable sieges of abdominal bloat and pain, accompanied by frequent, then almost never remitting, diarrhea. The sensible tack of a sensible man, of course, would have been to visit a clinic, be examined, given a diagnosis of whatever intestinal disease had been contracted, then treated.

But I was not a sensible man, and was rapidly passing beyond feeling the weary body my mind hauled around. For me, this sick body did not hurt; it *spoke*. The nausea, gut pain, explosive diarrhea were not a set of unpleasant symptoms but messages confirming my hated body's existence, like the sexual stirrings I had known and stamped down the autumn before. If I had hoped to displace my desiring, painful human body with one contrived from the dust of distorted memory, old photographs and such, the strategy no longer worked; the old body was asserting itself.

For any hypochondriac—guardian of an unreal body tormented by unreal symptoms—real disease is a nuisance. It is, usually, not lethal, merely troublesome, and hence puts the lie to the fantasy of that unseen, unfelt malignancy the hypochondriac wishes to believe growing within. Real disease exposes the psychical magic by which the mortal body of the radically distressed has been transformed from flesh into idea. To the soul-sick, physical disease is a matter of spirit and mind, as bloody filth is hemorrhaged from bowels of anxiety, a tangled network of filthy tubing more vast than any single human body could contain. To be neurotic is to imagine that the stench of diarrhea is the odour of mind.

---

13 July 1967

A wet night of blowing rain, dark fingers rattle the glass
in the old frames—
  the sickness keeps my secret clothes dirty, and the stink
is not secret sickness—and a blue light at the window,
then blackness, and the stink of filth in my clothes—
gone, the girders that traverse my brain, keep it from
rotting into a luminous puddle, leaking out into my
clothes—gone, the girders of penance, prayer—my
fingers are sick and weak, my feet dissolve and drizzle
into my guts, and out the weak ring of erogenous muscle
into my secret clothes—the stink of the earth I am, and
am losing, the ring is weakening under the weight of
stinking, pooling rot—

The oily liquid waste that gushed night and day into the toilet, reeking, filling me with hatred and disgust, seemed to *be* me, and *not* me; the essence of me, but only as one deteriorating part of a world turning from solid substance, discrete objects, into a tide of bloody feces flowing turgidly into my bowels, and out, uncontrollably.

As the world rotted into waste, it required a conduit, a runoff back into the cistern of itself; I had become that exit. As my natural heft disappeared into the toilet, my weight lost in the flux, I imagined that my body was disappearing—or, rather, all of it except the single ring of ruined muscle through which the liquefied earth poured out, back into its own mouth. I believed I had become the anus of the world.

The last month in Ireland was also the last, worst month of this liquefaction. It ended, as I imagined it would, just before I left behind the library, the bibliographical work I had set out to do, unfinished. I was headed back to university; for me, there had always been truth in the medieval superstition that one does not age during Mass—for which word substitute *university*. There, I would be safe from the ideas of death and disorder that had plagued me all summer—safe, too, from disease: a *mind only*, disembodied, disembowelled.

Arising before me, over the edge of the world, I jotted on foolscap pages during the late-August return flight from Shannon to New York, *a quiet year of avoidance, carefully delineated peace, detachment. Freedom from the nagging surge towards distracting involvements of every kind*.

Yet upon arriving at the university to proceed with doctoral work in literature—the most recent station on the *via dolorosa* of ever more advanced training in matters to which I had become indifferent—the stale peace after which I had been hankering began immediately eluding me. Sick with the bowel disorders of Ireland no longer, I became suffused with a yet more general sickness, a stillness, stagnation, a sense of slow, nauseating drift and dissolution.

I still could maintain a simulation of order in the papers written for courses, and, as well, in the bright clearings of seminars when busy talk was all that mattered. There were also hours when I forcibly lost myself in writings on *Beowulf,* Spenser, and Middle-English linguistics. But the sentences in my diaries were darkening, becoming contorted and disjunct, as I more and more scribbled tiny hates, grudges, dislikes and pains into the pages.

The first two of my three final academic semesters in graduate school passed as a waking dream, none of it needing recollection here. When I shuffle through the boxes of things that I have so carefully preserved from those two semesters, autumn, 1967, and spring, 1968, I find only a few notable objects, and even those I now want to destroy.

There are strange and malicious letters in the box, sentimental, forgiving notes, violent and menacing ones, obscene rants, sweet entreaties, all written and never sent to the elderly woman in Louisiana I believed to have been my father's last mistress. There is a note from the dean of the Irish cathedral, asking that I send him the cards I had compiled in the library, then promised, at the time of my departure, to order and complete upon returning to North America. The note prompts a suffocating memory of angrily, tearfully stuffing the worthless, wretched bibliographical scribblings into a cardboard box, staggering with the box to the post office through heavy snow, and sending the box away to Ireland, whereafter I never again heard from the dean.

And there are, of course, diaries—increasingly heretical, God-hating, human-hating diaries, pages where my leaking, fugitive mind hid itself in blasphemies.

---

early Christmas Day, 1967

    midnight
     after mass
     it-<u>body</u>
     it   it (<u>the body</u> is hungry again
     it must be fed or it annoys in the daytime
     it must have its erogenous nozzle drained
     it must have its nozzle fuck-jerked every day so the
    white fuck will spurt out and poison something else
    instead of poisoning my mind
     it must have its hole opened for the stink-corpse of
    food to come out and sink into the water standing in
    the toilet bowl

    i am 26
     or <u>the body is 26</u> and it and i were there at

The Holy Communion of Christmas
crack of bread smell of wine, smelling its way into
existence
swallowing me down and digesting me
soggy bread of flesh turning to shit and urine: this is
my body, this is my blood—
that is what i heard tonight

body
swallowed by music and clatter and jawing mouths
and the smell of it, the crack of it between rotting teeth
of myself—
thus done in and done out the back end of me
into dirty pants that have to be changed as soon as
I can be got home, and my hands must do the changing
of the pants because I cannot—and there is nothing in
the pants except the filth of me
the rattling sound of the starched place inside me is
fuck-sound
I know nothing except the pant the busy hand-jerk-
shuffle and dirty pants with white fuck poison in them
soaking into shit stains—my hands should be burned
off so I will not fuck-off myself any more, they should
be napalmed off—
me getting it in the was and being torn top to bottom
to pieces in the will be, hiding the white poison fuck
this is my blood, given for what, given for it, the body
and that is nothing

———

For the first time in almost thirty years, I have opened the dirty carton faithfully hauled from place to place, left unopened for a dozen good reasons. For the first time, I am reading these journals from the final year before the illness in them, within myself and the language of myself, finally overwhelmed me. What I find on the pages, what I remember of how they came to be made, is a clattering, broken loom spinning narratives and shreds, the shuttlecock madly flying back and forth inside a darkened room, stuttering out the winding-sheet woven from twisted, weakened threads of memory, from gossamer strands of histories, malevolent phrases. The will to keep myself chaste, to keep mended the barricades against intimacy, was weakening.

It is not easy to find a recognizable body of any sort in the tangle of texts from the autumn of 1967. Hateful words seem to spurt from nowhere against nothing, mutterings of self-directed malice prompted by some slip or mistake or slight I cannot now recall. A certain merciless gaze is fixed on the handwriting, an explicit and obsessive will to murder.

Yet, as I recall that year, there was something other than hatred dominating me. Hate, that is, was not yet the only desire dictating the work of the spinning-mill of being. There was another: the blasphemous mimicry that dragged me wearily through the postures and motions and linguistic gestures of academic "normality."

My attendance at classes continued, and was, at first, consistent. In the first semester, my essays and research papers still held together, receiving high praise. But from around Christmas onward, my academic offerings steadily diverged in quality. Some of it worsened, particularly when the job required the usual coherent exegesis of poem or novel, while the rest of it became queerly irradiated, luminously intelligent and free of my hitherto closely guarded pedantry. The latter papers earned a sort of fascinated admiration from professors who knew that such fractured, brilliantly glinting prose could only come from the oddity I was becoming.

Towards the end of the spring semester of 1968, I was failing a seminar on Middle-English literature that required the sort of assiduous attention to *Quellenforschung*, footnotes, rigorous linguistic analysis and parsing of which I was becoming incapable. I was still hanging on, however, in the lecture courses taught by the few professors who clearly recognized that I was tending irreversibly towards breakdown, but who saw light through the cracks of my creaking, contrived personality. Even as late as May, 1968, I still rose and dressed properly on Sunday mornings, dutifully went off to attend the Holy Eucharist at the nearby Episcopal cathedral, and behaved as correctly in public as my disorderly emotions would allow, keeping the hate and rage, violent erotic fantasies, the inner, exhausting revilings of self and God tightly confined to my diaries. I was enjoying the last firm grasp I would ever have on the lying poses of my divided self, the last buttoned-up modesty provided by the finely worked tapestry of fictions that served to conceal the hideous nakedness and disarrangement into which I was declining.

Apart from my family in distant Louisiana and Texas, among those least aware of my declining was the priest by whom I had been instructed before Confirmation. With him, I kept up a reasonable, uncomplaining correspondence. He remembered me from the days in 1966, when I had enjoyed the most emancipated love for the Church and for Christianity I would ever know. For even if it was the ceremonial and majestic history that engaged me most strongly then, the aura of establishment that comforted me in my discontent, something more—Someone else—other than neurotic escapism was drawing me towards the heart of the Church, and enlivening me in the process.

The priest remembered someone who was theologically enchanted, lively in practice and faith, because that was the person I let him see. All else in my riven and contradictory life— the psychic torments, the sexual misery—I kept secret; though, at least until the end of 1966, there was not much to keep secret. If depression was never far away, it was mitigated, for a time, by the newness, the loveliness, I was discovering in the Church.

I had never been a joiner; though in whatever groups or clubs I did join, I always strove for a certain conspicuous position, a recognition that I almost always got. Such was my experience in the months before my Confirmation, during which I made myself obvious in my Episcopal parish and in the group of Episcopalian university students who met regularly each Sunday afternoon. If my motives for joining the group were Sunday schoolish, nostalgic, part of the psychic programme of not growing up, the activities themselves were among the happiest I recall from this troubled epoch of my life.

So it was, during this involvement, that my enthusiasm for matters ecclesiastical came to the attention of this priest, the university chaplain, who appointed me representative to a national committee charged with advising the hierarchy of the Episcopal Church on its work among university students. As part of my new commission, I travelled to New York once every three months for committee meetings.

I was infinitely stiffer than my colleagues on the committee, many of whom were busily involved in the civil-rights and anti-war movements. But I loved those trips to New York, and the fresh, surprised radicalism of my fellows on the committee, I made acquaintances, as zealous as I could manage, with those from other universities, especially those enduring a familiar inner struggle between old family traditions and the lure of social action in the late 1960s.

At the committee's gatherings—practical and pious, tinged with strong skepticism towards all authority and established truth, and characterized by the same longing to go deeper that had always been the strongest of all my mixed motives for joining the Church—I became a different person, a happier one, than the tortured graduate student I was when in my rooms at university. So it happened, at our meeting in January, 1968, that the group chose me to travel to South Africa in the upcoming summer, to represent the Episcopal Church at various congresses of that country's Anglican student movement, then universally mobilized against apartheid. Another of my official jobs was the preparation of a report with recommendations for the Episcopal

Church's highest executive body, then seriously considering—against a strong counter-force from prominent Episcopal layperrsons in New York's financial industries—the withdrawal of the Church's huge investments in South Africa. (The Church eventually decided to shift its investments to "cleaner" companies outside South Africa.)

It seems my colleagues, and the head-office clergy who advised the committee, had no idea that, by that time, I was rapidly falling apart—that there was no reason to think I could psychologically survive a summer in Africa, much less do the work asked for. But how could they know? I was never happier, never more buoyant, than during those brief meetings in Manhattan—never closer to the sober Anglican sanity I had hoped would become for me a pattern of life.

———————

10 February 1968

*a tiny winged seed in empty air and the wind is bigger
than I am*

*a dying man, doing small, quick things on a quiet raft
drifting towards the falls*

a dying man doing

*perhaps and perhaps not someday, in the spring so far
away, an uproar of birds, roots, twigs rain (sky craps
snow now)*

*a dying man on quiet drift on snowy river, dying into
falls.*

*it woke me up. stiff tall stump between belly and the
bedsheets, blunt prow purple. lights wink on, up and
down the street.*

*fuck drying now on stomach now. on the hand
grasping this pen now. a drying smear of it on this
page—white clots in tangled hair nesting around limp
drying dick—*

> *a drifting man dying*
> *a doing raft drifting*
> *and a drying, a dying man empty as an old Mason jar,*
> *empty dick drying and dying fuck and raft*
> *snow*
> *night*
> *falls*

Of all the matters that must be dealt with in this charting of my life's disorder, no topic is more uncomfortable or more offensive to write of than the journey I made during the summer of 1968 throughout southern and central Africa.

This summer was the last before my breakdown the following autumn, and what I witnessed and what I did and did not do—almost certainly precipitated my final collapse. Yet, however numbing and disabling my pain, and though I had not yet discovered help at home, it was nevertheless available. There was no help for the leftist journalist I met in Durban, banned from writing, and stricken from the list of the living by the state, or for the Black priest, Anglican and activist, with whom I shared a hut at a youth conference in the Cape Province, a young man destined eventually to be murdered by the racist state's mysterious, thuggish police years before apartheid's crumbling.

And while I had increasingly experienced hatred, even suicidal hatred, towards my body, I had never witnessed hatred on such a scale, exercised with such irrefragable, slow and steady intensity. The very fabric of social life in the Republic of South Africa was continual malice, renewed each day by fear omnipresent, omniscient secret police and a huge public bureaucracy existing only to enforce the irrational race and anti-subversion laws. Most insidious, however, was the continual whisper inside the head of every South African warning of the revenge awaiting those who transgressed *the boundaries,* whether ideological or geographical, sexual, social, abstractly legalistic. They were sometimes obscure or indefinite, these boundaries, but always dangerously near.

I learned of South Africa in conversations with outright victims of bigotry, smooth accommodationists with pleasantly guilty consciences, principled racists, daring opponents of the regime, souls mangled and crushed into acidic cynicism, right-thinking folk resigned uncomfortably to their prosperity attained within the System, the apolitical, the political, the post-political. And it was precisely during these conversations, while being schooled in South Africa's culture of coordinated, chromatic and subtle terror, that the hand of mine that held the scripts of "normality" finally began to shake uncontrollably.

The scripts were, and are, easily come by. They precede us, are *there*, always, for us to pick up and use, or not pick up, forming a library of possibilities that rings our existence like the horizon.

For most people, it is the master-script called "normality" that is adopted, the sum of codes and strategies required to avoid punishment and exclusion, to get what and where we want. In the case of some of us, however, the attempted adoption of the master-script is disrupted in mid-transmission by some physical or psychic rupture, leaving a scribbled, incoherent message on the spirit. A portion of one's performance in the world, one's being, is left primitive and liquid, either unshaped by language or shaped by garbled lines. For such persons, being in the world is an act in the purely theatrical sense, a series of readings delivered uncomfortably, but with whatever conviction is allowed by the individual's skill, ambition, acting ability, deviousness.

In my case, the accurate delivery of the master-script had always been painful, exhausting. It was made possible by the indulgence of others, and by the fact that I was white, male, a graduate student on my way to respectable professionalism—and hence eligible for the deference still accorded young men in the proto-feminist 1960s. Thus were my shabby renditions of civil "normality" taken for the real thing, by almost everyone.

The reason for presenting a liberal-democratic façade to the world, of course, was to conceal, as fully as possible, the backstage hammering and nailing together of a murderous fascist state within. How dearly I wanted to establish such a state within myself, to hold the crumbling bits of propriety together, did not make itself manifest until South Africa.

Upon arriving there in early June, 1968, and being received graciously by the beleaguered Anglican resistance to apartheid, I gradually began to enjoy the awareness that, for the first time in my life—at least since rejecting the racist American South for what I took to be the "liberal humanism" of Northern high culture—I had discovered a place that required no play-acting of "normality," at least not of the bourgeois-democratic sort I had learned to affect.

The tale narrated by my Anglican colleagues—of publicly sanctioned absolute control of one group over another, and an oppressive madness that had become the hallowed and official ideology of the state—was received by me with an outward show of concern and dismay, but, inside, with a deepening sense of contentment. I had come at last to a world I understood, and in which I felt immediate citizenship. It was a zone of quiet, total war, waged mercilessly and continuously by the empowered against the powerless, by the pure, rational, ideological mind against the undocile body.

Of course, there was no question of what side I would be on in this war: the side of the powerful Sexless against the impotent Sexed, the White against the Black—adjectives which, in ordinary South African parlance, were still wholly charged with ancient connotations of purity and evil, honour and pollution, reason and irrationality, all incontestably opposed to each other. This, then, was the paradox of that summer. Sent by a magnanimous, famously humanitarian American church to represent its interests, to affirm its solidarity with the oppressed and their defenders, its emissary found himself genuinely happy only among the racists, the anti-Christian totalitarians, the suppressers of the innocent.

For in the company of such people, and in their company only, I
was able to throw away the hated script of "normality," to go as
mad as they from blind malice and prim rectitude—to become at
last pure and pleasureless, an agent of innocent hate.

The smooth, rationalized madness, or my reception into it, came
closest not in South Africa, but in the tiny monarchy of
Swaziland, pressed like a dry pea between the vast pillows of South
Africa and Mozambique, still a colony of fascist Portugal in 1968.

Because of its proximity to Johannesburg, a centre for white
anti-apartheid criticism, Swaziland had become a place of quick
refuge for South African dissenters, especially Communists who
had openly defied the regime until they were turned into hunted
criminals by the passage of fierce anti-Communist legislation. By
an odd coincidence, it was in Swaziland that I saw for the first
time the truth of South Africa—or, more precisely, the truth of
the aligned southern-African regimes who exercised terror continually while trying to keep this terror hidden from everyone,
citizens and outsiders alike.

The revealing episode began during after-dinner coffee and
dessert at the home of an elderly, prosperous medical doctor, her
grey hair cinched back into a tight little bun—a white South
African, as it happened, who had fled minutes after a tip-off
from comrades that the police were on their way to her
Johannesburg home. It was the end of an evening I had found
especially congenial. The doctor was a Communist of the attractive, old school—*mitteleuropäische*, Jewish and secular and
sophisticated, the creator of a tiny, gracefully cluttered Viennese
apartment, situated improbably in the midst of black Africa.

I was about to leave this haven of antique furniture and sweet
porcelain and return to my bare tourist hotel when the doctor's
telephone rang. Upon answering it, and listening in silence for a
moment, she became agitated, then began to weep. She asked
me if I would drive her that night, immediately, to the

Mozambique border, since her age and poor eyesight prevented her from motoring on the lonely, dusty highways after dark. Everything, she said, would be explained on the way.

As we hurtled on bumpy roads through the blackness of the African night, across the high east-African plateau between her house and the border post, she told me the tale of a friend, a Red comrade, an engineer until his forced flight from the South African secret police. A janitor in a Swazi school ever since, and miserably unhappy, he had acquired a false British passport, transit visa and enough personalized odds and ends to make him seem to be the person he claimed to be.

His strategy involved stealing from Swaziland into Mozambique disguised as a fusty, faintly confused British tourist on a grand tour of the former Empire, making his way to Lourenço Marques, headquarters of Mozambique's colonial administration and its principal air terminal, then escaping Africa by plane to London.

Waiting for him at the airport in Lourenço Marques, however, were the Portuguese secret police, told to expect him, almost certainly, by their South African counterparts. The man had been apprehended, immediately identified, and physically and mentally tormented into admitting his ploy. Thereafter he was deposited at the principal crossing into Swaziland, a tiny boxy building by the side of a dirt highway, where Portuguese officials threw him across the line. From that desolate place, he had telephoned friends, who in turn had called the doctor; and in that place, he waited for us to take him from the brief, vivid hell he had just endured back to the more permanent, infinitely boring one he had sought to escape.

What we found upon arriving was a man morally and emotionally crushed by his failure and by the force unleashed against him, left battered and trembling by physical abuse. As we drove fast over the uneven road back towards the heart of Swaziland, he sat crumpled in the back seat, sobbing miserably, crying out again and again that he would never get out.

Here was evidence of entrapment of a kind I had never known. But here also was reality of the sort I avoided at all costs—that all neurotics avoid: the abrupt fall upon one's body and consciousness of the Other, in all its careless, suffering, bull-powerful and unforgiving Otherness. Yet perhaps because I had become so practised in preventing these crashes into the guarded secrecy at the centre—or because something had gone dead in me, or never been alive—I felt nothing. No compassion, none of the ordinary embarrassment that could be expected when closed inside a car with a sobbing, broken stranger. No curiosity about the victim's wounds, nor any concern about his future.

Nor did I feel anything very early that morning, after the trip back. I merely could not sleep, so I went for a short walk around the hotel grounds, down into the dirt streets of the town. It was then that I looked up, and noticed, for the first time since I had arrived south of the equator, that all the stars were different.

I had arrived, I felt, on a different planet, one friendlier to the violence raging inside me, with different heavens and a different ground, one inscribed with hatred and soaked in blood. Were I to remain here, within the genially totalitarian web of relations, in charge of dispensing even a little menace or terror, I would be happy. There would be no need for further dissimulation, no more keeping-up of liberal appearances.

I kept my feelings secret that night. I kept them secret the next day, nourishing them privately as the little Air Swazi plane skimmed the desolate veldt, taking me back into South Africa. Only towards the end of the flight did a certain feeling begin to bloom on the stem of my thorny little secret—something so frightening, unsettling that I could not write about it, even in the coded diaries I was keeping. The scent of that blossom was erotic, unsettlingly sexual, brutal, sadistic.

Instead of sympathy for the unfortunate man I had found on the Swazi-Mozambique border the night before, my dark, warm desiring went instead beyond the stark frontier station where the doctor and I had found and received the man's tortured body. My desire travelled imaginatively farther still, towards the nameless, faceless powers deep inside South Africa and Mozambique, who could know anything, do anything they pleased to anyone, who existed only to ruin unimportant people attempting a pitiful escape. What stirred me was the awareness that, all they did, these powers did without remorse or pity or sorrow.

I longed to go into that night's darkness, to seek out the infinite powers and surrender to them, to make common cause with them in their stupendous mission of enforcing nothing, sustaining continuous repression of mind, body, loyalty—to take part, in whatever way they would allow, in the unfelt tormenting of the obnoxious sons by the all-knowing fathers. The pleasure I felt oozed from the fantasy of standing by while these powers unleashed pure force against a naked, helpless body from no motive other than the casual desire for pleasureless obliteration.

---

mid-July, 1968

   *i felt nothing   nothing in the drive through the African
night*
    *nothing at the border   nothing when the man got
into the car   nothing about his broken body his broken
spirit   nothing*
     a cup of tea, a cup of coffee, thank you, no thank you.
     a body broken   the man sobbing in the back seat
   while i drove through the African night i did not care
     it does not matter a cup of tea a cup of coffee
     thank you   i feel nothing   i cannot smell the fuck
   on my hands
     a cup of tea a cup of coffee
     all the stars were strange.

The last decline into dissolution came early in that autumn of 1968, after I had returned to graduate school in America. I could read almost nothing. The words seemed to blur, or burn themselves painfully into the back of my eyes. I could write nothing, keep no notes in class, because I could not hear. All was occluded by the rattling of chains, weapons, hatreds and memories in my brain—by the uncontrollable flickering before my eyes of memories and pseudo-memories from childhood, Africa, Ireland, anywhere. I was plagued by sexual arousal when I remembered Africa, dreaded erections when my mind drifted, beyond my control, to the sight of the broken man in the back seat, suffocation when I remembered Ireland, my failure to complete the neat bibliographical project there, that summer of 1967's rain-soaked sorrow, semen-stained sheets and underwear, hatred of books.

Of all that happened before I finally fell apart, most painful was the close-down of senses, the blinding and deafening, even though my hands were on the ropes drawing up the bridges and lowering the gates. This pain was to save me by eventually making my situation untenably desperate—but not yet. I still deeply longed to create a tiny South Africa inside my body, as a last defence against marauding desires, distractions, rebellions.

It was not until much later that I realized that depression is the culture of such a society writ small: the self as a tiny modern state, mimicking the totalitarian state's boredom and frantic distraction, oppressive and parasitic bureaucracies, police forces, its terror that leaves no visible scars. Our intimacies are conducted like foreign policy. The depressive issues contradictory demands to himself, practises seductions meant to subdue and degrade and control others, and unruly forces inside the self. At the heart of our policy is, of course, the modern state's greatest arrogation, its ultimate power over us: the *right to judicial murder*. Suicide is capital punishment under another name.

But that understanding would come later. In the fall of 1968, I only knew the distance yawning ever wider between myself and whatever I thought the world was. I believed I willed my deafness;

in any case, I could not hear what was being said in seminars and lectures; my notes were scrambled texts, inchoate, obscene. Yet despite the general deafness, I thought I could make out certain words there, in the distance—all hostile, malicious, directed against me, and focused on my ruin. There were whispers in hallways, mockeries of me, my stupidity and brittle correctness. Smiles on the faces of professors I happened to encounter in common-room or class were condescending sneers, communicating hatred of me with every glance.

With growing preoccupation, I imagined myself stalked, surrounded, conspired against. In the end, I decided my enemies were trying to kill me. I went downtown, to a shabby army-navy surplus store, and, as a defence, bought a steel knife with a needle-like point and razor-sharp blade. This knife I kept always near me, tucked into my briefcase during classes, hidden under piles of books in the library, sheathed and in my coat pocket when I went on night walks. I could not sleep without the knife on the bed-table, to protect myself from the enemies in the event that they should come for me at night.

In that fear there was also desire, that an enemy *would* steal into my room, giving me the reason to complete my vengeance against my enemies: to slash and mutilate the oppressor, to bury the knife in soft flesh up to its steel hilt.

When the other enemies did not come at night, I was left with the only enemy who never left me—and my thoughts would then turn to slashing myself, hacking open my filthy bowels and letting the bloody feces flow into the sheets until the bleeding and the flowing stopped, leaving me dead, quiet at last, peacefully asleep, no longer fearful. The desire for self-slaughter burned in me most intensely when I masturbated with no fantasy save that of plunging the knife into my abdomen, destroying phallus and mind and body and gut at the same time, ending memory and mind and life in one obscene spill and absence.

———————

early September, 1968

Amazing, the bilious ease with which the first days of class go by, the slippery time of nothing said, nothing heard—my ears are stopped

how the silent images go by on the screen in my mind, mouthing nothings to me, doing nothings.

i lie naked on the sheets, fan blowing cool air across nakedness, drying the fuck, cold, still wet in clots of sparse belly-hair—hate, noisy rage inside, louder than the rattling fan—

outside on the sheets, belly spotted with hated fuck, fuck-spurt hate—inside, stampeding of hate for them all—nothing worth living for but the hate, and there was enough of that tonight at the "graduate students' cocktail party"—i hated every stupid moment of it, every stupid smiling face.

"What are you doing this fall?"

Nothing. Doing fuck-jerk, empty squirt poisoning the sheets. blood.

"What are you doing?"

Being thing, getting nothing. Being knives in darkness, haunting the soft bellies and slashing them open. Hating the university as I have never hated it before—knowing vile things, coming up from the stink marshes in the bottom of myself, hateful things, ideas of revenge and hate, murder by fuck poison, seeing all of them, the people who run the feudal hierarchy of English—dead, fuck-smeared poisoned, dissolving bone and fat in vats of corrosive nothing, and nothing beyond that—

In the real world I was abandoning, there was indeed a secret conspiracy afoot, intended to do me good.

My professors were growing increasingly concerned about my

odd behaviour, specifically my unprecedented, repeated failure
to perform with even bare competence in seminars and classes.
Late in the autumn of 1968, the department decided to act; and
I was politely and firmly told by the head of graduate studies
that it was the university's opinion that I should withdraw from
doctoral studies at once. In the opinion of my teachers, he told
me, I was well on my way to a complete mental breakdown, and
no longer capable of academic work. He told me to get help.

I left the university at once, finding temporary refuge in the
New York home of acquaintances, an Episcopal priest and his
family. My final exit from university did not, however, happen
quite as quickly as the head and his cohorts wanted. One of my
professors, a remote, terse teacher of modern American literature
named William Rueckert, unpopularly interested in Freud and the
French structuralists, had not been previously told of the department head's decision to recommend my withdrawal, and was outraged about it. He insisted, successfully, that I be asked to return
from New York, re-enrol, and finish the term, which had only two
months more to run—because, as he told them, an instantaneous
break from the secluded, disciplined schedule of academic life, and
flight into nothing, could well prove disastrous to me. He also
pointed out that, while failing at many things, I had produced
perhaps the most creative, experimentally thoughtful papers of my
academic career. After just a few days in New York, I was recalled
to my studies, saved by Rueckert from almost sure destruction.

This helpful professor was, and is today, an outsider by dis-
position and an outsider by choice. In my university days, he was
not an easy person to get close to, even for those who were captivated by his fresh readings of old texts and his improbable
awareness of foreign ideas in a graduate English department
antipathetically American. I admired him, but I cannot say I ever
really knew him; and I had no idea he was as committed to me
as he turned out to be.

After I somehow finished the autumn term—by which time
I was definitely in no shape to continue—he made one final

communication with me: a page photocopied from a book and dropped into the mail, without comment. The book was an examination of the recurring breakdowns of the poet Theodore Roethke, which terrified him as much as they did those around him. Roethke's psychiatrists during these devastating depressions dwelt at length on the silence that fell upon the poet, his inability to write or speak coherently. But on the page Mr. Rueckert sent me, the author of the study pointed out the fact that always kept slipping past the doctors: after every descent into near-madness, Roethke's poetry was stronger than it had ever been, his creativity more abundant. Or, as the author put it, Roethke's periodic "disintegration" was part of a cycle that always involved "reintegration at a higher level."

The text hastened the hateful, dreaded decision to turn myself over to the mind doctors, though my principal reason for doing so was that I could think of nothing else to do. Exhausted by my struggle merely to feed and clothe myself, I went for psychiatric testing at the famous teaching hospital attached to the university. After an assessment I remember little about, and the determination by the social worker who interviewed me that I was not merely trying to dodge military call-up and Vietnam by playing crazy, I became a case.

---

14 November 1968

vicious days
  the dogs—tearers, attackers
of the lost and sick—
    cowards in the darkness of the bush—
jackals haunt the necropolis, round the tombs of the
dead, piss on once-white walls

  assassinated, i foul the pavement with my rot,
excrement of death   ruining the dirt with poison

*the dogs prowl in the mind, ready to destroy—to kill
in befriending—to murder in loving—*

Now: love the dogs no longer

CHAPTER *3*

Underworlds

December, 1968

David (after our first meeting:
pill, drug, something you take for a headache or
schismatic life...
   glue

---

*T**he** objective miseries of my initiation into psychotherapy were several: the initial interview with a bureaucrat, the wait for unseen powers to make a decision about my "treatment," the further wait for the first session with a psychiatrist, the descent into the unknowable. But far worse than the clinical procedures of admission was the burden of self-perception as moral failure. If this sense of lapse pervades, to some degree, in the minds of perhaps all prospective patients today, it weighed far more heavily in 1968. It is true that orthodox mind-doctoring of the sort dispensed by ordinary hospitals and clinics was then under fire from psychiatrists on the fringe of the profession, and from a few patients brave enough to speak out against their mistreatment and the uncontrolled psychiatric dictatorship that allowed it. In 1968, however, standard mind-medicine was still wreathed in the postwar aura of virtually irresistible authority almost incomprehensible today, but which then imbued it with both horror and fascination in the public imagination.

On the one hand, I was horrified by the notion of surrendering to the doctors—because of the confession of failure such surrender would involve, and because I believed that, once in their clutches, there would be no escape. (For persons more deeply ill than I was in the 1960s, that fear was certainly not ungrounded.) On the other, I could no longer contain the oozing of rage and corrosive fluids into speech and behaviour; I longed to have my incoherent body put into a jar, under militant, watchful authority, lest I spill again, attracting the slavering attention of the black dogs, which I felt closing in to destroy me once and for all.

I had reached a standstill by the autumn of 1968, frozen by fear of going down either avenue open to me—"seeking help," as going to doctors was called in those days, and not seeking help. My decision to go to the vast campus hospital was due, in large part, to the exhausted supply of ears to whine into, and the decision of my academic department to send me away. But it was also grounded in the image I had of doctoring: the establishment that had rapidly, entirely and with what seemed like miraculous efficiency eradicated my generation's childhood terror of poliomyelitis. It seemed to me a social power capable of alleviating any disorder, any symptom, including the terrifying forces then freely wreaking havoc on my language and action. I found myself longing to stand under the gaze of pure power, the penetrating spotlight of absolute knowledge. I was ready to become a "patient," the melancholy atheist I had always feared depression would make of me—a willing object, isolated before the technologies of psychiatry, language, power.

18 December 1968

My liturgy, ritual: to rend the categories of body,
snatching apart the body of Osiris so the scraps can be
found and become a god—i am Osiris in the papyrus
swamp, torn limb from limb by my demon brother,
demon Other—
i would return from stasis, deadness, with a billion
names burning inside me—Osiris once whole, then
sundered, then stitched together by Isis in the papyrus
swamp, a patchwork of radiant names, all different—

My case was adjudged serious. It had been immediately assigned, and I had been notified of my first appointment. The hospital functionary who called me said the name of my therapist would be presented to me upon arrival at the clinic.

The days before the first hour of psychotherapy—an hour destined to spin out into years, then decades of being a patient—were suffused with obsessive thoughts of blood, my bleeding and self-torment, alternating with hours of motionless, outraged stupefaction.

I could not rinse the blood from my mind, nor drain myself of the hatred of my body for failing the test of self-cure. Though I did not know his name, I already hated the therapist to whom I had been assigned, inasmuch as he represented for me the visible, frangible symbol of that failure. In the whirl of contorted logic that filled those days, I made up my mind to hate him and submit abjectly to him at the same time, to secretly despise the world to which he belonged—the world of "normals," "successfuls"—because it was the very world from which I felt excluded.

Checking in at the front desk of the vast research hospital, I readied my words. I would speak of blood and savagery, of self-slaughter, of the merciless absences that kept me awake for nights on end, of hoping to draw down upon myself the .obliterating therapeutic powers I believed would bring my confusions from darkness into daylight, for extinction.

———————

After politely introducing himself, David said he was a post-doctoral student in psychiatry, our sessions would cost five dollars an hour, he would probably be seeing me, at least initially, every weekday, and he would be audiotaping our sessions for use in meetings with his academic adviser. He asked me nothing.

David's detached, institutional manner, his apparent lack of concern, annoyed me. But it was his announced intention to tape our discussions that most deeply offended. I had imagined our meetings would be entirely between the two of us, with no eavesdropping. If my self-training in the compression of hate into a tiny, radioactive malignancy within me had been failing lately—hence the odd behaviours and shut-down of hearing and seeing that prompted the request that I leave graduate school—I recovered it enough, that first day, *not* to show indignation.

The first session was business-like, and remained so without interference by me; David played the dispenser of administrative information, and I played the good student and listener. I fancied he would soon ask me a question, perhaps inquire as to what seemed to be the problem. Instead, David announced that time was up, and that he would see me the next morning at the same time. He did not say goodbye.

The irritations of the first hour were nothing compared with those of the second hour, the next morning. I again assumed David would surely ask me what was troubling me, and start giving me the clues to unplug the drum of seething hate and hurt inside my mind. Instead, he began by quietly asking what I believed would happen between us, and how we should proceed from that understanding. The questions took me aback. The process of psychotherapy, at least as I understood it, was supposed to be about helping *me*, not deciding on a contract between *us*.

If what I understood suggests a very fundamental ignorance of the processes inherent in psychotherapy or psychoanalysis, it's true: I knew nothing of the drama beyond what one can glean from Hitchcock's *Spellbound* and from graduate-school essays on Freudian approaches to literature. It was a stance of belligerent, deliberately vengeful ignorance, not uncommon, I imagine, among those who can least afford such ignorance.

I had deliberately avoided knowing anything about "analysis," because it was, to my mind, a fashionably *American* thing to do, and something nearly all the urban, affluent young east-coast Americans in my graduate seminars had done, some in childhood, nearly all in adolescence. Neurosis, as I understood the word, was less a life-choking disease than a certain quirkiness designed to drive their appallingly bourgeois parents insane, and "therapy" was merely an expensive dumb-show played out by manipulative children for the benefit of their hand-wringing parents.

It was the snobbery—or the fear masquerading as snobbery embedded in my Southern-Gothic hostility towards everything upstartish and Yankee—that, at bottom, had delayed my learning anything concrete about the dynamic exchange of therapy. Though familiar with the basic texts, tracts, studies and case histories written by Sigmund Freud—such reading was *de rigueur* in my graduate-school circles—I had made no practical connection between anything on the page and anything possible, desirable, in life. Even the public lectures of Norman O. Brown, then a professor at my university—*Life Against Death* and the poetically encrypted, sensuously radical *Love's Body* had just appeared—had meant nothing to me, beyond the merely informational.

The real reasons that I did not allow, could not allow, Freud's words to come alive for me lay in my disorder, which neutralizes all harrowing language that could expose it. What I told myself was that Freud's apocalyptic discoveries, if apocalyptic they were, had undergone such dilution, such suburbanization, that "analysis" itself was now nothing other than a balm for the show-offishly wealthy.

Despite my dislike of David's question about "what would happen," and because I had been primed by depression to submit obediently to those who possessed something I wanted to get, I felt obliged to give an answer. So I said something about disclosing difficult things, very terrible things buried deep in my wretched past; confessing secrets never told to anyone. I hoped that, armed with the knowledge of this unhappy past, he would identify my disorder and prescribe medicine for it, in the form of insights about my problem. In possession of these insights—tools, rather like screwdrivers, putty knives, wrenches—I would then be able to repair the cracking façade, shore up the failing defences against my enemies, and get on with graduate studies.

David said nothing. He simply gazed at me, and jotted down something on his notepaper, and said our time was up.

---

25 December 1968

> *hateful reality tides over the beach of me, saturating*
> *bodily tissues with inert facticity, hardening and*
> *hurting—i have no erotic fantasies, no happy ones*
> *anyway—i want them, bright and warm not bloody*
> *and violent, dissolving crystallized facts displacing*
> *organs and tissues and mind inside me with cold*
> *bright stone—*

i hate david for being soft and quiet, while I jerk
my stone cracking body around, creak and gush tears,
seepage from mind, piss and white stinking fuck
staining underwear, leaking anus, leaking mind...

What I did not then understand, perhaps could not have understood except in an abstract way, was that psychotherapy is very largely a matter of disappointment and bad friendship.

Good friends sympathize, are malleable to a degree, are willing to fulfil, up to a point, our need for companionship. Psychotherapists refuse to be malleable; they firmly, unemotionally decline frantic requests for information, compassion, even ordinary kindness. They go away on holidays or to conferences exactly when we do not wish them to; yet they also flatly refuse to cancel sessions at those inevitable times we feel "cured," in no need whatever of their consistent disrespect.

Walking out through the doors of the clinic into the deepening winter during the earliest weeks with David, I imagined, with increasing fear and urgency, that he simply did not respect me enough to hand over his secrets. My task, then, was to make him understand the importance of my case and of myself, the hurry I was in to get back to graduate school, medicated with the purges necessary to free my body from the sodden, heavy hate dragging it down. I was, in my view, a special case, deserving better, quicker treatment than David was prepared to give me. I came from an old and notable family, I brought him an unusual, dark history unlike anything he had heard before, and I was prepared to offer him those terrible stories that had shaped my consciousness and ruined my grasp on whatever pleasures existed in the world—narratives from which he had the power to unlock me, if I could persuade him to do so.

It was not very many days before David at last asked me to tell him about myself. So began the unrolling of the dolorous carpet of tales, with its pictures of me, depressed to a deathly degree after the quick vanishing of my father and the horrible fading of my mother; me, the small scion of Southern country gentry, ruined by the move to the democratic, bourgeois town; me, crazed by the arising of sexual desire, suppressing it in the name of perpetual virginity, yet finding the pent-up urges distorting and deranging the smooth surface of my life; me, onanist with mind filled with violent thoughts, spilling seed into my fist when what I longed to do was spill the blood of my imagined enemies.

I listed at length symptoms common to virtually all depression—though I did not know then that my complaints were anything but unique. I complained of a decline in vital energy; a weakened ability to enjoy the fulfilment of needs or of aesthetic desire. Even the most reasonable goals had become difficult or impossible to set, and, when established, impossible to fulfil. I was continually shadowed by the sense of being busy going no place; most psychiatric patients, I imagine, are shadowed by the same oppressive feeling.

I complained about sleep troubles, eating troubles. I found myself avoiding all but the most urgently necessary contact with other people. The ill feeling that, for some depressives, does not get much worse than a generalized unhappiness would in my case often degenerate into overwhelming self-loathing, climaxing in sudden, surprising relief, or thoughts of suicide.

All around the world, doctors in research clinics write down the words that patients use, and the words, in turn, are added to a list of symptoms in the clinical handbook. They become the topics we discuss in that peculiar sort of conversation and transaction known as psychotherapy, even as their use turns a depressed man or woman into a clinical topic, or a candidate for the discourse of depression.

If you have not found out before your first visit to a psychiatrist, you quickly learn how to become an object of clinical concern. You listen to the psychiatrist's or social worker's questions during the initial interview. Are you often sad without sufficient cause? Do you have trouble concentrating? Do you avoid others? Why do you look as though you are about to start crying? Answer all these questions truthfully, as any honest depressive must, and you become *something* in the eyes of another human being. A tinker, a tailor, a candlestick-maker. Or a depressive.

I do not wish to sound as though I am belittling this early stage in psychotherapy. Indeed, becoming something with existential status in the troubled, drifting bourgeois world from which most psychiatric patients come brings with it intrinsic rewards—even if that *something* is a neurotic tied in knots so tight that the consolations of friends, drugs and alcohol, even affection, cannot unsnood. At last, one *belongs*. And the knowledge that one belongs, if only to the tribe of neurotics, brings with it an experience of farewell to nothingness and anomie, and embrace by a special society with rules, restrictions, requirements, and, above all, an etiquette for living in a larger world that, by and large, has abandoned etiquette. The talk-treatment of depressives is very much a learning of this etiquette, not from a book but from intensely regimented conversations, hedged all round by *dos* and *don'ts* more strict than anything in Amy Vanderbilt. One comes to psychotherapy with what amounts to bad manners, with ugly rules of playing the game that are stoutly adhered to, even when they repeatedly bring down defeat on the one trying to play the intricate sport of civilized behaviour.

But all that, I would learn much later. In the beginning, I unfurled my banner of bloody symptoms flamboyantly, since I believed these details would engage David's interest and lure him more quickly to the point of handing over the information I wanted. I rehearsed carefully before each session—though the more assiduously I practised, the less effect my performances seemed to have. David merely listened, apparently unmoved, and resolutely "unhelpful." He did not grimace in dismay, weep with me; he did not extend sympathy, or express regret, or even smile in derision. In fact, he did nothing and said little until he announced that "time is up."

As the wintry weeks passed, boring me infinitely—I could do nothing but sit alone in my apartment and cycle each day to the hospital and home again—the stories' tone began to change from matter-of-fact, only occasionally punctuated by tearful interludes and choked silences, to increasingly dramatic, and then to rapturously melodramatic, self-punishing, self-condemning. Yet nothing in David's countenance changed. His silences frustrated me unspeakably, yet I continued to nurse my grudges in secret, expressing my rage at him only as rage at myself.

As my histrionic bid to get sympathy tottered and failed, it gradually, troublesomely began to dawn on me that I might well be unable to overcome this stranger's powers of resistance. With this awakening to powerlessness came a steady worsening of every depressive symptom. The symptoms, in turn, produced a dramatic increase in new things to say, even as the pathetic old stories were becoming boring, blunted tools useless for anything. Rushing each morning into his little, bare hospital cubbyhole, with its pale green walls and linoleum floors, I would go over with David the past twenty-three hours of heightened symptoms: acute anxiety, an inability to walk outside my apartment for any reason except *this* one and food, a further thickening of the walls between my soul and the world.

All the while, I would be thinking: *this time he'll listen, understand.* But at the end of the fifty minutes, David would still be sitting there listening, but otherwise ungiving, apparently unreceiving.

---

24 February 1969

*Returned to my apartment from a party at Larry's place,
which I despised, walking through cold and snow, and
thinking with midnight mind...Houses with a few lights*

on behind brown paper shades—the chiaroscuro of
shadows cast by street-light glare, plays on the snow
of sharp black shadows, the souls of rattling branches,
all bare of leaves now—
*   midnight sights, but no midnight sounds—and the*
absence of sounds reminded me of the violence awaiting
the people in the houses when they awaken from their
sleeping walk across the night-bridge, awaken into the
morning, and the violence at the end of it—
*   Perhaps they were awake, making love in the light*
behind the paper—then they would sleep, and cross the
bridge to the violence—
*   Walking in the snow, deep on the Clarissa Street*
bridge—points of city lights shattered on the black surge
of river water—and slipping in seemed so easy then—
a ripple, then nothing under the broken flashes of city
lights shattered on the black toiling—water tending
beyond here, always tending beyond, never staying—
bearing off the bright shatters of light and the body into
the darkness beyond the city, towards whatever sea it
yearns for, to be lost in—

In the weeks of therapy that followed my initial encounters with David, I was visited by quickening pain, seeming to turn ever more deadly. As the incessant rattling of self-punishing thoughts became deafening, the paralysis of will I had come to the clinic with seemed to become exaggerated. I could do less and less: shop, socialize with any peace, go to entertainments other than movies, and then always alone. At the same time, the focus on myself sharpened. This self-centredness became obsessive, then sickening, then oddly consoling—inasmuch as I believed myself at last on the clear way towards death, my father, the silence. I dwelt much of the time on suicide; or, to be more accurate, on the melodramatic swoon and theatrics of dying.

This morbid, ethereal absorption did not then lead me to *plan* suicide, for the thoughts I had of it were plainly too pleasurably aesthetic to be interrupted by impudent reality. Yet they did have the effect of blinding me to two other insults to my disorder and history, both visited upon me during my visits to David's tiny office.

One was his presence there every morning when I arrived, not in order to give advice, nor telling me why he, or I, was there. He was not, however, behaving in the same fashion as nearly everyone else in my adult life: listening intently a while, then losing interest, gradually withdrawing, finally vanishing. David simply *would not die*, as my father had died and vanished, and the others had died, withdrawing—perhaps not because they wanted to, but because I refused to participate in any scenario that did not conclude with the death of the listener.

Another transgression perpetrated by David's silence and his indifference was a gradual, hurtful dragging of my attention away from myself towards him. I became obsessed by him—with an obsession compounded of confused outrage and erotic curiosity, revulsion and fascination, all of it intense, cross-wired, contradictory. I thought of nothing, nobody else. Day after exhausting day, I would return, never daring miss an appointment—even while realizing that nothing would break the field of impassivity David maintained around himself, resisting every manipulation on my part to make him respond to me.

———

Had I understood what I had read of Freud, I would immediately have recognized the onset of this vexatious emotional passage. Since Freud first observed it in his clinical practice and famously described it, theorists of the psychiatric transaction have called this typical, intensifying attraction and revulsion *transference*. The metaphorics of the word are banal and baldly bureaucratic; a person *transfers*, for example, from one university to another.

But even if we found a more colourful, less technocratic name for it, the phenomenon is real, predictable and dangerous. According to Freud, in any case, the quanta being furtively "transferred" to the doctor are, presumably, the anciently repressed energies of love and hatred that the patient has harboured, undisclosed even to himself, towards a person or persons whom the codifiers of civilized behaviour have stricken from the list of candidates for erotic love or passionate hatred. (The list is, of course, headed by closest blood kin: one's father or mother, sister or brother.)

As early as 1909, Freud was finding that this attachment of feeling by patient to therapist happened "every time that we treat a neurotic psychoanalytically." The patient "applies to the person of the physician a great amount of tender emotion, often mixed with enmity, which has no foundation in any real relation and must be derived in every respect from the old wish-fancies of the patient which have become unconscious." Here is psychotherapy's crucial, most curious component: the intense desire that therapy seems to release in the patient, yet is kept deliberately at bay, unresolved and volatile by the psychiatrist's unshakable equanimity, secrecy, non-involvement.

In this story, the looming figure of the Father, among Freud's most durable (and, unfortunately, most trivialized) contributions to the modernist iconology of emerging selfhood, is the "object" of the patient's wish-fancies. Now it's all an allegorical fairy tale, as Freud himself explains with characteristic flair in his masterpiece *A General Introduction to Psychoanalysis*: "Given that a case can be successfully cured by establishing and then resolving a powerful father-transference to the person of the physician, it would not follow that the patient had previously suffered in this way from an unconscious attachment of the libido to his father. The father-transference is only the battlefield on which we conquer and take the libido prisoner; the patient's libido has been drawn hither away from other 'positions.'"

Put into words within Freud's metaphor, but closer in tone to the imbalance, dread and confusion of depression, life is so many repetitions of a doomed resistance *to becoming one's own father.* To do so would be to cease being the victimized child, and become the author, or father, of our own human destiny, with all involved in becoming human: sex, intimacy, ordinary courtesy, predictable honesty, a resting in vulnerability, richness of choice, the reach and the instructive pain of rejection.

It would be an insult to Freud's poetic subtlety to lay all my troubles at the feet of my *biological* father. It is in my contract with culture, specifically with the fathering operations of civilization, that the problem lies. The remarkable event of transference condenses this conflicting whirl of affection and fear into a focused interchange, a *situation* in which two human beings are locked in a battle of mastery. On the battlefield thus created— Freud's image is both superb and apt—my energies came to be directed towards one end: gaining and controlling David's love for me. But had David actually "loved" me as I wanted him to— becoming yet another ear to whine into—then the end of therapy would be doomed to remain forever frustrated: the ridding myself of these very stultifying, paralyzing scripts and routines that, so long as they were effective, had driven me ever deeper into loneliness, and to near-despair of life itself.

Each time an outbreak of emotional theatrics or self-pitying weeping crashed into his stony countenance, the armour that had been suffocating and killing my spirit was being weakened and dismantled. I was furious. At the beginning and afterwards—I am not free of this twisted reaction even now—I turned the fury against myself, punishing myself for feelings I did not understand, and believed myself forbidden to have. Gradually, I sensed I could, and then I did, complain bitterly to David about his unresponsiveness, his unhelpful passivity— things for which I had never before dared reproach anyone. What I did not understand was that this anger had already begun, little by little, to set me free.

The gift of real emotion, even anger, is the working of a wonder, the creation of a setting in which a patient can allow genuine feeling into a human interchange. If I was angry with David, and said so, I was at least making the first honest contact in a lifetime of concealed angers, suffocated emotions. It would be many years before I understood—if I really understand it today—that this first course of psychotherapy was not a pro-gramme of cure. No repair of the damage done by depression took place in the body-shop of the psychiatric interview room. And the intellectual insights every intelligent neurotic expects to gain from therapy, as a reward and right, are disappointingly few, if any come at all. To use Freud's pleasantly pedagogic metaphor in the *Introductory Lectures*, therapy was "re-education"—an intense, uncanny, radical relearning how to walk, act and feel without the shabby and dilapidated scripts fashioned over a lifetime, and now being rendered powerless in the therapeutic interchange.

----

24 April 1969

*dense day in the mind's terrain—sky lowers, full of
monsters risen out of the body's sea—paralyzing
fantasies, spinning me away into illusions, damning
myths—we can only love in myths, in the myths we
are—*
     do not leave me father do not leave me alone....

26 April 1969

*"you are going to have to learn to live without your
father. you are going to have to accept your father's
death": these were sentences David spoke to me....*

This encounter on the libidinal battlefield with David was shot through with danger, real and mortal. Even now, even with the help of my diaries, I cannot untangle the stories, separate the several shudders that shook me to the foundations. The day may never come when I will recollect clearly those turbulent days, nor when the bewitchments and punishments clustered in memory will ever be drained wholly away. Psychotherapy has not performed the miracle of turning an infinite, interminable grief, a loss of worlds into a finite act of mourning.

But inside David's room, I recall, the words were emerging ever more slowly, the ruptures in the trains of logic and discourse becoming more frequent, more distressing. And in the world outside the clinic, which I had hitherto been able to keep more or less separate, came the same stutter, stammer as inside it. My armour, the armour of language, was failing. Even short trips to the corner store left me exhausted by the nearly unbearable labour of keeping my psychic nakedness covered, as the armour broke off with clangs I alone heard, leaving chinks and jagged holes everywhere. I felt the presence of black dogs in every alley, around every corner, waiting to attack, tear and feed. Even behind the triple-locked door of my apartment I did not feel safe from their approach. Fearing the peaceable sleep they bring before they kill, I stayed awake until dawn, then slept until nine, the hour when I had to leave for my next meeting with David, the next incident of ruin.

Then came the April morning, unforgettable, when David gave me perhaps his only direct admonition: to cut, deliberately and consciously, the sinews that had kept my father's corpse lashed to my back throughout all the years since his death. By this point in my history with David, my biological father was not under discussion, but rather the strange, diseased, tumourously growing homunculus I called my father, created to fill the emptiness left by his absence. In this thing, I kept paternity confined, so I did not have to grow up; into it, I could put the erotic, libidinal movements of growing up, enabling me to remain a virginal, inert child in my Gothic tale forever.

To unhitch my "father" from my back, to bury my muttering, punishing invention; or to die: these were my alternatives, a proposition revealed with a clarity I had never known before. After months of almost ceaseless turmoil, tears and unnerving pain, a fine calm descended upon me, pacific and cool as a gentle autumnal dusk; and I knew what must be done.

With something approaching prayerful devotion, patient and unhurrying, I planned the suicide. I visited the medical school library, studied diagrams of the vascular system with methodical pedantry and weighed the options. At the end of this study, I decided on the exact location of the incisions, the methods of making them that would kill most quickly, effectively, and be least susceptible to reversal should I be found before dead. I bought the tools.

On the appointed night, the gleaming new knives were ready, laid out with a surgeon's precision on the flat edge of the bathtub. There would be no mistake. This would not be a reshoot of the New Year's Eve scene in *Sunset Boulevard*, when the faded film star Norma Desmond slashes her wrists in a way that makes quite a show of blood, and attracts much attention and pity, by a method that probably cannot kill anyone.

The black dogs had worked their magic of peace. The distractions were gone, my mind clear and free to concentrate with descending calm on the destruction of the nothingness I had become.

Exactly how I arrived, or anyone arrives, at this point of calm, in which self-mutilation loses its ordinary revulsion, I cannot say. But Freud's exquisitely poetic observations of suffering in *Mourning and Melancholia* ring true to me here.

In both mourning and in its pathological shadow, melancholy, Freud finds "a profoundly painful dejection, abrogation of interest in the outside world, the loss of the capacity to love, inquisitional of all activity, and a lowering of the self-regarding feelings to a degree that finds utterance in self-reproaches and self-reviling, and culminates in a delusional expectation of punishment."

In the end, however, the mourner abrogates the treaties of life with the one now dead, releases the loved one into death, thus ending what Freud famously entitled "the work of mourning"—but only "bit by bit, under great expense of time."

If the work of mourning is not done, as, in my case, it had not been, the rage against withdrawal is driven into the dark underworld of the self, to twist and gnaw and become eventually a thing no longer recognizable as sorrow. The *melancholic* is Freud's designation of a person who refuses to shed healing tears. He "displays something...which is lacking in grief—an extraordinary fall in his self-esteem, an impoverishment of his ego on a grand scale. In grief the world becomes poor and empty; in melancholia it is the ego itself [that becomes poor and empty]."

But what is the engine driving this self-hatred, obsessing the melancholic with his "bodily infirmity, ugliness, weakness, social inferiority"? Freud's conclusion: these self-reproaches are in fact reproaches against a loved one, "shifted on to the patient's own ego."

The proof of this contention—blasphemous to intuition and common sense, as well as to the melancholic's manifest intent of holding on to love—need not concern us here. It is enough to say that, with no knowledge of *Mourning and Melancholia*, with indeed no knowledge of the dangerous script Freud describes and I faithfully followed, I was in fact moving in slow, tedious dance-like motions towards ultimate self-punishment. Ahead of me loomed the acknowledgement that my self-disgust was in fact disgust for my father; that the brutality I wished to inflict on myself was a wound I would inflict on him for damning me to grow up in one family that hated me because I was the son of their daughter's tormentor, and another family devoted to me solely as a virginal, pure replacement for the wretched son they had lost to alcohol and women.

The absurd way of life one assumes to avoid releasing the dead father is melancholia, or what is now called depression. The absurd finale towards which it tends is always suicide: murder of the hated one misdirected against the self.

———————

I recall being abruptly shaken out of self-murderous bliss that night by a blessed jolt of repulsion—a glancing reflection of my face in the bathroom mirror seems to have had something to do with it; or perhaps some other force of which I know nothing. But I wanted to be where David was, or could be found; and that was the emergency ward of the teaching hospital. After my examination, admission and sedation, I passed into dreamless sleep.

To my mixed shame and relief, David came to visit me the next morning. In the stillness of the hospital room, he listened with the usual impassivity and fixed attention. I could not kill my father, I said; I could not bury him. I would rather die myself, to be with him.

Again, with his usual oddity of manner, he merely replied that, were I actually to attempt suicide and survive it, "our relationship would change." He did not specify what that change would entail. He then left, abandoning me to bewilderment; but in this bewildered state, I sensed a new fear, even greater than the fear of losing my father: the fear of losing David.

For the first time, I felt dawning within me a shift of loyalties. Slowly and obscurely, I decided my curious friendship with the living person of David, though limited and difficult, was preferable to the care of my dead father's body. Throughout that stay in the hospital, I turned over and over in my mind the novel thought that I would rather be with an unpredictable, living, remote man than a dead one wholly under my control. Only in this strange new life would form-giving be found, strong hands to stitch together the fragments of what I was, into something new.

———————

16 May 1969

i will be forgiven for what i have to do

———

*beloved father, whom i would protect because you are
myself, in me: you must be buried now*
*you were, then you were not, and i sought you in the
days and nights*
*alone in my bed i cried myself to sleep for years, always
wanting you, to be your boy through the years—and
when the time came to seek another's body i could not
because of you—so i sought you in the days and in the
nights, in the men and women in the nights, and they
were not you*
now you are beyond harm, so beyond protection
*father in whose arms i would stay, beside whose body
i would remain forever,*
you are dead and now comes time for burial

Shortly after my release from hospital, a graduate-school acquaintance dropped by my apartment, uninvited. As neurotics will, I grasped at this opportunity to talk about myself, but quickly found myself stumbling into silence. So, to fill the unnerving silence, my visitor began telling tales of his recent erotic adventures and misadventures with women, laughing at his own folly.

I had always found (and still find) sexual image-spinning and dirty jokes repulsive. And, more to the point, I had no direct knowledge of sex. In any case, the stories saddened me and I began to cry the scanty, embarrassing tears of the depressed, whereupon my bewildered colleague left—but not before kindling in me a spark of a terrorless imagination of sex.

Following this episode I began to talk with David about sex—the actual having of it, doing it, and having not done it. If I did not know it at the time, I was accepting intimacy as a right of existence. The obstructing corpse of my father had to be loosed to make intimacy possible, or at least thinkable. While the intimacy germinating in my transactions with David was still intensely important, it began to be boring. I wanted more. I didn't want to be virgin any longer.

───────────

The moment did not come at once, though it came perhaps as simply and quickly as it always does, when a man or a woman is ready to leave virginity behind. Along the way towards that end, however, came an event—outwardly banal, yet vivid and blessed in my memory—worth telling about, even if my recollection will probably mean very little to the reader who has not known the special apartness of depression.

It happened on an ordinary shopping street, in spring. I was walking around, going nowhere in particular, when, ahead of me, a young man crossed the street. I had never seen him; nor did I experience any sexual desire towards him. A man was simply crossing the street.

This ordinary event became pentecostal only because it awakened in me a sensation I had never had: a sighting of another person that I knew, ultimately, was not unlike me. Whatever secrets and desires were hidden in the mind behind his face, the heart beneath his plaid shirt, they were like mine; or at least were not foreign to me. For the first time outside the encounter with David, I knew the freedom and distance of another person without fear. That recognition of communality and remoteness, his and mine, fell upon me with blinding immediacy, and with exquisite joy.

───────────

Without the simple insight into freedom this incident provided me, I possibly could never have accepted intimacy without possession, the utter subjugation, the penetrating knowledge, of the other. At some less psychologically idiosyncratic level, I was at the same time discovering belatedly what every normal boy and man knows: the force of this wish to fall from dubious innocence into the unpredictable complicities of intimacy.

The Italian writer Guido Ceronetti tells us that "a medieval sentence defends the rights of the penis: *Quod turget, urget*—What swells, impels. It sternly equates these rights with those of the abscess and the pimple." I was learning in my last days of virginity something close to what Ceronetti had in mind, the ordinary community of pimple and penis in at least one respect: their urgencies, independent of mind—their rights, like those of the man crossing the street. Carnal desire *belonged*; I was learning that.

My first sexual proposal was met, first, with surprise, then polite rejection. Yet this rebuke, which might have wounded me only months before, I brushed aside and quickly went on—*quod turget, urget*—to the next person I could think of who might be interested in being my Virgil in the sexual underworld.

Deborah was a strikingly beautiful psychiatric out-patient at the hospital, and, when her disarray permitted it, a student at the university. She was almost incandescently intelligent in those sane moments granted her between plunges into delusion.

We had been drawn together as psychiatric out-patients often are, I suspect, by the poverty of things to talk about, other than disorders, doctors, treatments. If our lot was forged in common interests in philosophy and literature, we also shared the knowledge that, when our disorders permitted, we could talk about writing and thought; and when they did not, no explanations were necessary. Our hours of sane conversation were luminous; our hours of silence were blessed, unharried. Waiting in the hospital's neon-lit lobby to welcome Deborah after one of her seasons inside, after shock treatments or deep sedations, was perhaps my first act of genuine, eager friendship.

Deborah imagined me to be an outcast and a loner forever, as thoroughly excluded from continuous happiness and normal joys as she believed herself to be. I now know she was mistaken. I was ill, and had little hope of being whole. But, in every sense, my depressive condition was negligible compared with Deborah's. From the onset of her disease, Deborah was already beyond what little help the doctors could then give.

If we miscomprehended our disorders, we did not misunderstand our attraction for each other. My interest lay in her dark physical beauty, and in her knowledgeable citizenship in the netherworld of the counter-culture, of which I knew practically nothing, to which she introduced me. Her interest in me was similarly carnal and curious. So I proposed we have sex—just like that, without euphemism or modesty.

———————

25 July 1969

> *the men and women I have made love to in the mind,*
> *the ghostly corpses of men and women in my sexual*
> *fantasies—the ghostly men and women i have used,*
> *supine, dead, unfree—I used these for years because*
> *I could not find living people dead enough to use—*
> *I remember the shame, falling on me in Indiana, when*
> *I was caught in my fantasies of having him—and now,*
> *no grandiose schemes, no elaborate salvation devices in*
> *my head, no more savings, but real having at last—*
>   *Manuel Bandiera: "Let your body come to understand*
> */ another body / Because bodies, unlike souls,*
> *understand / each other."*

———————

Throughout the Saturday before my evening date with Deborah—I cannot recall any of this without a smile—I mentally rehearsed again and again how things would be managed, how this would get into that.

My sources were not very numerous. I had never talked with other males about *doing* sex. Hence, I relied on the few movies I had seen as an adult—which almost, but never quite, showed what I wanted to know. I also had the somewhat oblique information found in the "boys only" sex books my grandmother had given me in adolescence; and almost nothing else.

The evening in bed thus turned out to be less rapturous than exploratory—an adult version of Playing Doctor—though the surge of delight, when it happened, was as stunningly interesting as the books said it would be. Mostly, however, I was glad to have gotten it right, since ensuring that the etiquette of something is got right—such is my misfortune—has always been more important to me than obtaining an astonishing result. Be that as it may, sex happened, as happily and as easily for both of us, as completely devoid of solemnity and embarrassment as I could have hoped.

On the Sunday morning after that first carnal teasing and caressing and arousal, union, *jouissance*, I woke up earlier than Deborah. The first light of that summer dawn, seeping through the dingy window-panes of the student rooming-house where she lived, rinsed her naked body and mine and the white sheets under us in blue.

As I lay in the dim half-light of the peaceful room, sleepy and happy and quite pleased with myself, everything seemed right. Except for one thing. I wanted to talk about it. But not with Deborah, with whom I had shared this first erotic intimacy of my life; that would have been too normal for me. I wanted to talk to David.

On Monday morning, he greeted the stumbling, euphoric description of my sexual encounter with the same unsmiling, silent impassivity with which he had waited for uncontrollable crying to give way to speech. This time, however, his quietude was tinged by an unwanted concern, which I took as patronizing. I thought my therapist, if anyone, should have been proud of me, like a parent when his ugliest duckling gets a date for the dance. He was not even slightly proud. He was concerned, I came to understand, that a certain seed of optimism might have been planted in my mind—the notion, perhaps, that I had been *cured*; that this single night had prepared me to throw myself into the real world.

He was right to be concerned, since I did believe that. For months, virtually my every gesture and communication had been within a therapeutic environment. My symptoms, crises in transference, descents into blinding depression, struggles back to the surface had become the stuff of my life, my conversation. But his worry was not merely that I would imagine myself cured. He also saw that I would likely incorporate sex into therapy—using it, not to start breaking the heavy bonds that linked us, but to give us something new, rich, interesting to talk about. As David knew, he was the person I was in love with; to be near him, I would go on inventing stories forever, inventing exploits, having crises and breakthroughs. He was right: sex with Deborah had been a performance *for him.*

---

late July, 1969

> *"the universe is made of stories, not of atoms"*—Muriel
> *Rukeyser, in* The Speed of Darkness, *IX*—
>   *biography, "life-writing"—also a matter of making a*
> *life from stories, creating—and, like God on the first*
> *day, making mistakes in calculating how much freedom*
> *we could bear, blotting the copy book before the writing*
> *begins, making obsessive deletions, little erasures and*
> *tiny, moment-by-moment suicides in the text—*

Looking back over my left shoulder at the mad-making moons of that spring and summer of 1969, I find that distance and the years have gradually leached away the pain of my mistakes, the sadness I felt upon discovering how misdirected my hatreds or my affections had been. I get a kind of lazy joy from thinking about those events—the sort people experience, I suppose, when musing idly, forgetfully, on the days of carefree youth. Having never known any such days, I take my suspect pleasures in the *density* of 1969—the squeeze of language in therapy that began cracking the imprisoning fear of intimacy, and the first-fruits of that freedom.

Nevertheless, I was navigating deep water, the danger of which was known only to David at the time. I do not know why I did not run aground and perish, or why I have not perished since, since my illness has not been cured. There is no cure; only recurrences of that crisis called a *nervous breakdown*. The term has always struck me as strange, pale. The experience is less one of breakdown than of crowding, or nausea; a rupture in some psychic bowel.

I should nonetheless be glad to call this event a "nervous breakdown," were it not for the phrase's suffusion with late-Victorian ideas that seem foreign to whatever I went through. In the picture conjured by the words, the word *nerve* lies hidden in adjectival darkness, its ambiguous meanings shifting like the lights on quicksilver. The ancients conjectured, without proof, that a spangle of sensitive fibres radiated from and terminated within the brain. Yet before they were discovered to be physiological realities, nerves had passed from conjecture into metaphor, attracting overtones destined not to disappear when the actual system of neurotransmission was discovered and demonstrated.

What exactly is it, to have a nervous breakdown? In the very first instance, it is to be tangled in a web of metaphors unsimplified since Victorian times. "Occasionally conveying an idea of courage and vigor," writes psychiatric historian Janet Oppenheim of the Victorians, "[nerves] more often stood for fragility and weakness. They suggested sensitivity, sympathy, and, above all, a suffering that frequently defied medical knowledge and curative skill." The evasive idea of *nervous breakdown* still spreads miasmically between physiology and culture. It is an intensely painful, disabling disorder confined to an individual body and self—an empirical snapping and misfiring of nerves, that is; but it is also the snapping of one's fidelity to a set of social codes and behaviours defined as "normal," "natural." The precise linguistic structures of self-hatred belong, and will always belong, to the order of culture, not of physiology.

But in ways now dimly understood, our bodies can prepare us for the nervous breakdown's discourse of self-hate. Though flatly contrary to commonsensical notions of the body, the mangling and disabling of neural structures by traumas that do not otherwise harm the body is now unarguable physiological fact. Disorders in the neural templates and circuits may not *cause* nervous breakdowns, but they almost certainly *invite* ready-made cultural vocabularies and behaviours of loathing.

Of course, certain events that get called nervous breakdowns are almost certainly *not* psychological but purely physical diseases, like a brain tumour, with nothing cultural about them. In the case of the British novelist Arthur Christopher Benson, Janet Oppenheim tells us his collapse was accompanied by, in his description, "a persistent sleeplessness, a perpetual dejection, amounting at times to an intolerable mental anguish." But his mental state was "perfectly unclouded and absolutely hopeless." That is *not* what I have ever experienced as depression. The hopelessness has always been accompanied by a wracking of the mind, a wreckage of the ability to think clearly about anything.

Nothing, of course, can reverse the history one has built while under the influence of the aversions, fears and stultifying emotional death of depression. As psychiatry was to discover in this century, the scripts the depressed write to live by can almost certainly not be unwritten, and are very hard to rewrite. But it may well be that someday, in a society less obsessed with wellness and a hankering for untroubled subjectivity—a culture resigned, as ours is not, to the ancient truth that only what can be broken can become whole—the so-called nervous breakdown will become a ritual opening to health and larger life, a crisis in a slow, terrible build-up of distress caused by obsolete notions and words, and the start of a requilting of the peculiarly human blanket we call culture. In the meantime, the twentieth century has come up with at least one strange ritual, characterized by the peculiarity and uncanniness so common in rites of passage to higher levels of integrated spirit. It is psychotherapy.

A man entered this fearful transaction at the end of 1968, and endured a partial smashing of his worthless sentences, his incantations of self-hate. He would never come permanently from this ritual passage through the underworld.

But one morning in the late spring of 1969, he did drop his knife into the river.

And on another morning, he awoke naked, satisfied and happy, and gazed without greed or malice at a sleeping woman's breasts.

CHAPTER 4

Border Crossings

Jean-Paul Sartre once remarked, with perhaps less fidelity to fact than to poetry, that "there is no such thing as the psychological. Let us say that one can improve the biography of a person."

Our biographies can indeed be improved, as mine has been improved; but never rewritten. There will always be within the biography of a depressive a *small gap* between seeming and reality, a little lie within every transaction in the world, a lingering suspicion that whatever nearness, friendship, erotic love we experience are only simulations of realities we can never know. This is true, because we know the world only as unreal, insubstantial, working according to agendas that are always secret. But surely that perception, in turn, is grounded in another: that we are unreal, however "improved." If having sex with Deborah that first night of many was for David, to give me a reason to go on in psychotherapy with him, then can any depressive's agenda be explicit?

I do not know the answer. But this I know: if we forget the black dogs for a moment, in sex or some other pleasure, they never forget us. Even when we think ourselves most perfectly hidden, most happy, they will seek and find us, bringing their stony realism to crush our fugitive belief that we can write ourselves out of depression's script forever.

But as for little rewritings, small deletions and erasures, rearrangements of the text? Yes: they are possible to do—or so I am inclined to think, when thinking back to 1969, and about my biography since.

---

3 November 1969

<u>*homo faber:*</u>
   i write on the first page in a new-bound book, first scrawling furrow in the thawed field—the ploughman is very old and brings young seed—
   —the grounded Ark's attic door is not yet open—in Noah's trash and treasure is the wisdom, but how to find it, when the door is not yet open and all the past dissolves in light—a journal is a field bounded by stonepiles to mark a passing, or the site on Ararat the Ark's bottom scraped, came to rest, treasures old and new tumbling from it onto spring-moist mountain field—
   Allen Ginsberg said tonight: "to ease the pain of living, everything else a drunken dumbshow"—the terrorized little boy must now be unafraid, words not used as weapons, but as fingers for the touching, the sort, a

shuffling of the Greater Trumps and their fateful
laying—

The telephone call from a professor named Paul Levine came late on a spring night in 1969. I sat alone in the old red wingback to which I had always retreated in the maddest hours, sickened by speaking into the darkness and by the wild scampering dance of thoughts in my head. The voice on the other end of the line was the calm voice of a respected teacher of literature, uttering calm words about matters I could hardly understand. They had to do—they *must* have had to do—with an invitation to move to Toronto, and teach with him in a new university there, leading little seminars extracted from the large audiences of lectures Levine had been hired to give.

I do not remember my exact reply. But at some time in the midst of cutting the corpse of the Edwardian boy from my back, there was an interview with Levine, a bus-ride to Toronto for an interview there with someone I did not know. There were letters, an agreement, perhaps more than one agreement. My diaries are silent on these events, for reasons I cannot explain, except that they did not seem to be happening, at least to me. But in the course of these incidents, I found I had a job for the next three years, teaching first-year cultural studies with Paul Levine in Toronto.

In time, Levine would come to despise his job in Toronto and return to Europe, where he had studied and taught years before. He then disappeared from my life altogether—without my asking him how fully he had been aware, in the spring of 1969, of my crippled ability to think continuous, coherent thoughts, and without my thanking him for the kindness of rescuing me from graduate studies. I shall never know to what extent his taking me on was an act of kindness. But whatever Levine's motives, his offer was the bridge to a new life and to a new city, and metropolitan existence, I have never, throughout twenty-five years, regretted embracing.

I arrived in Toronto by bus one afternoon in early August, 1969, only days after every force carrying me through the wretchedness of the previous winter and spring had broken, climaxed, collapsed—after first sex, and my last hour with David. What few possessions I had brought along, including my red-plush mad chair, were deposited in the flat I had found and absent-mindedly rented in a comfortably professional neighbourhood north of the downtown towers. With the exhaustions and ruptures of the move came exhilaration, all to do with *firsts*: first job and first pay-cheque, first apartment outside a student ghetto, first sustained venture into a genuinely big city, first spring on to a broad highway after eight months of travelling only that narrow bicycle trail between apartment and hospital.

There came with these excitements something akin to amnesia. Gazing into the flames on the hearth of my flat one unseasonably cool summer's night, I began to fancy that my gradual deterioration, the decline of mere unhappiness into narrowly violent self-destruction, all the trepidations and futilities, were now behind me. Even if life became rocky again, I had oars to steady my boat—what *they* might be, I did not closely question—and I would not come so close to sinking again.

I did not realize that as I looked into the flames, thoughts adrift on fragrant smoke and flickering light, the black dogs were gathering in the shadows behind me. A cozy, deadly feeling of safety enveloped me as I drifted off to sleep in my red chair—a soothing sense that the abrupt move from one city and country to another, from a zone in which there had been little but unhappiness to one wholly unknown, would simply delete the old anxiety and ungrounding, the scattered concentration, the snarling hounds of depression that had so often returned to snatch away pleasures, days, the ordinary grieving and mending.

It would be years before I abandoned the hope of a permanent alleviation of depression—if I have ever really done so, in the secret, stubborn corners of my heart. It was only a matter of weeks before the black dogs made their return, mocking my attempts at escape, terrorizing me with their unsleeping endurance. The thrill and distraction of those first days in Toronto wore off, giving way almost at once to the erotic and intellectual loneliness I had known in the last days of graduate school. Back came the immobilizing doubt and self-hatred, the peculiar suffocating anxiety that left me weeping by the heap of dead ashes in the fireplace and listening again and again to the same record, hearing nothing. Depression had come to Toronto with me, I discovered, packed in the locker of my soul.

David had given me the name and telephone number of a famous psychiatrist in Toronto, and had written him on my behalf. This was surely the only genuinely bad turn my first therapist ever gave me. After a brief spell of meetings in the late summer of 1969 with this self-important fool, I simply never went back. For the next weeks and months, and beyond, I tried to find David again, always *him*, in the offices of dim, dull and unmemorable psychologists and psychiatrists and social workers. With them, I found sympathy, the odd insight; but no new strength for staying the swift advances and retreats of the black dogs, the unremitting dull ache of unwellness, settling.

Yet I was nevertheless learning one crucial thing: there would never be another David. For even if I could return to the same man, and begin again a course of psychotherapy with him, there would be no more *me*, as I had existed in that wrenching moment early in 1969. The slide ever downward had been dramatically arrested, just before my plunge over the edge of it.

Upon pitching up in Toronto, I began to cycle through the ordinary pattern of depression that has remained more or less constant throughout my life since that time: swift or slow drifts into hurt, desolation and shame, into the darkness of hours or days or weeks at the bottom, the desperate hunt for help from drugs or therapists, the slow or rapid returns to the plateau of stability. Then always has come the going-on, with its flashes of fugitive pleasure and sometimes intervals of not unpleasurable hobbling forward, and the next stumble, slip and fall.

I did not yet understand that I was coming from *critical* depression into the cycles of *normal* depression. But I did not think about it much. So much was going on, just then: the disorientation of my first months in Toronto was intense, tumultuous, full of surprises, many of them pulled *on* me *by* me, but some quite unexpected. My job, leading seminars for two masters, involved me in the lives of both Paul Levine and William Irwin Thompson, old-fashioned sophisticates uneasily abroad on the streets of sliding, shimmering contemporary culture. The intellectual tension between these two volatile and ambitious dandies—Levine, a modernist, pessimist, secularist; Thompson, a McLuhanesque techno-populist speculator, self-anointed prophet of an impending Dark Age in which he had been ordained to preserve "the ancient wisdom"—caught all their teaching assistants in its sparkling, menacing dazzle.

But returning home after an autumn day of listening to their provocative lectures, and leading tutorials designed to probe deeper into the cultural issues raised in these deliverances, I found myself becoming mired in that foggy slough of dullness that the black dogs find so congenial for their watching and hunting. I wrote it down to loneliness. Even to newcomers with no previous history of mental disorder, Toronto is famously cold, unwelcoming. My aloneness in this city where I knew only my two remote mentors—the intellectual, sexual, social isolation of it— kept me continually off balance, increasingly inside. Sitting by the fireplace, I nursed the usual hurts and resentments that come from a depressive's unwillingness to venture anything untried, despite the self-hatred that results from exactly that inactivity.

Eventually, I met a couple of graduate students who seemed more comfortable to be around than most people I was encountering. Or, if not exactly comfortable, then at least recognizable: for these "student radicals," living in a run-down rooming-house and spouting bright Marxist cultural analysis, were little different

from the intelligent "movement" people I had known in graduate
school, and marched with against the war in Vietnam. And so it
happened that, by Christmas, 1969, I had upped and left my first
apartment and solitude, and joined my new-found friends and
their comrades in the "commune"—a name, preposterous in its
grandiose allusions to Paris in 1869 and to the China of the
Cultural Revolution, commonly given to "radical" rooming-houses
by their denizens in those failing, fading days of student protest.

late November, 1969

> *—on the decision to leave deer park and move in with
> the communists: nothing to be said—*
> *—on the great blue whales, which did not return to
> their breeding grounds this year; Ginsberg told us that—*
> *—on the terrific darkness and in it the radiance—I do
> not know what to write, there is nothing here to do, but
> the determination of way to satori, staying in it—but
> now there is the dark wood, the wandering...perhaps the
> new living with the communists on carlton street will be
> the right going, discipline, sufficient for now—*

The "commune" was in a tall Victorian house in a neighbourhood respectable a half-century before, by 1969 a shabby district
littered with drunks, addicts, down-and-outs of various sorts,
and us, that is, the communards: a couple of smart "marxist-
leninist" graduate students, a "community organizer" or two, and
some petty criminals whose idea of fighting The Capitalist
System was to deal dope, drop acid every weekend and steal
other people's yogurt from the fridge. And me.

My attraction to Marxism had always involved a naïve worship of its revelations, particularly the quieting of the matter-
babble of ordinary life, to disclose the engines of power churning

at the heart of pleasure, the knowledge industry, the spectacle of mass culture. Marxism had provided the first powerful diagnostics of culture I had ever known; I did not yet know there were others even more thunderous in their explanatory power, even if true to contemporary human being, and hence pessimistic, in a way Marxism never is. I had not yet discovered, that is, the writings of Martin Heidegger, or of Michel Foucault.

But having been provisionally baptized into cultural Marxism, at least as practised by the rooming-house comrades, my intellectual reasons for joining fled, and I quickly came to despise everything about the commune. It dawned on me that my isolation in a posh suburb had driven me into even greater isolation in the slums, and my move from a respectable neighbourhood into a musty student rooming-house—the sort of place, after all, I had found sexual intimacy the first time, in another city—had left me more alone than at any time since the terrible months before the crash of November, 1968.

Occasional visits from Deborah, my first and, until that point, only sexual friend, distracted and pleased me for a night or a weekend, relieving the grinding tiresomeness, the weight of ideological prattle felt not just by me, I believe, but by all those thrown together in the commune. A sense of desperate sadness and futility hung heavy over the house, its activities, even its busy, vociferous political bickerings.

The unspoken truth in the house was that the revolution now seemed ever farther away, "imperialism" more solidly entrenched than ever before, the suffocating miasma of mass-cultural distractions more deeply penetrating, more *commanding*, than it had seemed before the Marxist philosophers told us it existed. There was to be no overthrow of the state, not even a sweeping reorganization of the universities by radical students (as there had been in France), no instauration of ebullient liberty.

Nor, I suspect, was revolution deeply wanted any more by most communards, though nobody would have dared admit it. By the early 1970s, the day was past when anyone on the left, however "anti-Stalinist," could plead ignorance about the atrocities that so effortlessly, naturally followed the Leninist revolution, as day follows night. Similarly, there were very few who could be found to defend the tyrannical figure of Castro, the revolutionary hero favoured by comfortable North American radicals in the early 1960s. Even before the disaster of Sandinista Nicaragua—the last fantasy holiday destination for North American "radicals" in search of at least one Marxist revolution that did *not* fail, that did *not* murder its children and its finest minds—my comrades were quietly giving up.

Slowly emerging in the minds of us children of the dizzily optimistic 1960s, in various ways and with various effects, was the baleful truth about Enlightenment: that the train of events from liberationist and emancipatory rhetoric, to revolution, thence to horror and terror, is inevitable. Every depressed person knows that steady stalk-forward, from obsessive self-improvement and "pulling yourself together," to thoughts of suicide, which is merely the unleashing of Jacobinism against a body that refuses to be revolutionized. If few young Marxists—or "neo-Marxists," as they then fashionably called themselves—could admit to the consequences so clearly embedded in the prattle of liberation, they were (like me) finding ways out of it.

Deborah was my only refuge from the pervading sense of failure that hung in heavy funereal swags over every window in the house. When she left to return home, to the university hospital and her therapist in the city of our meeting, I was plunged back into the sickening aloneness, fraught with deepening self-hatred—the heavy sense of having made another wrong turn, a leap into the wrong place—and a pervading sense of disgust at myself and my decisions. The world had begun to slip from my grasp again, this time more grievously than at any time since the year before breakdown.

---

17 March 1970

> *St Patrick's Day 1970, memories of Ireland, 1967—a*
> *day to look into the grave of my heart, its hungers intact,*
> *seeking the community of the hearth. And what else?*
> *God is the name of it—God, timeless silence, the*
> *absence of clocks, caesura in the centre of the pulsing*
> *stress-forward of this death in life—God is the questing*
> *beast seeking the hearth's heat inside me, God the*
> *absence and the end, God the putting-away of the*
> *fears, and then the fall into God, light-sundered*
> *uncertainty—*

The next snap came as quickly as every other one during the intense seasons between the autumn of 1968 and—a time with its own tales, yet to be told—the summer of 1971. Wandering aimlessly, miserably around Toronto on the late afternoon of the Easter Day of 1970, I found a small Anglican church on a downtown side street, and discovered that I was on time for the Solemn Evensong of the Resurrection.

I had not been to church since Africa, almost two years before. One reason had to do with the intense shame, that never left me, of finding myself secretly siding with oppressors and degraders—the very people whose victims I had been sent by the Church to find ways to defend. The more compelling reason, however, was the disarray, the final step into the chaotic prelude to healing, into which I tumbled headlong after the summer of 1968 in Africa. But, as I was to discover, I had to abandon the Church in order to find it; to discover how much of the Church's attraction had to do merely with the cramped traditionalism and propriety I craved, and how much with liberating, living faith.

During the splendid liturgy at this church, the answer came. That evening, I knew again the beauty that had been the attraction, years before, in the solemn splendour of music and the pageantry—spared in no Anglican church at Easter-time, and at this parish church indulged in marvellously, lavishly and lovingly. But what I felt in all this were warmths I had known before most strongly in sexual intimacy with Deborah: the simplicity of being enfleshed, mortal, needy; the freedom, and the letting-go; the strange, new sense of *not* being a stranger, either to want or to fulfilment.

And behind the clouds of incense, the shimmering of gold vestments and the glories of music—the erotics of religion—was the still more wonderful loveliness of the Beloved, at hand among his people. The profligate forgiveness and welcome I felt in the radiant fabric of signs and sounds, in the fragrant skein of language incomparably beautiful, stood in high relief against the grimly serious Marxist maxims and exhortations, covering everything in the commune with a light, slippery film, like grease.

The Evensong was an aesthetic experience; I would never deny that. But what I felt was less contrived beauty than *aesthesis* in the ancient Greek sense: the sensual awakening that opens us to larger moral worlds. For to behold the Cross is to face a choice: to seize life, to remain with the Beloved in the darkness at noon and the utter uncertainty of that terrible Good Friday; or to retreat back into the bourgeois parodies of life—placid relativism, casual disbelief, the pathology of everyday life.

On that Easter Sunday, as in the years during which I was being drawn into Anglicanism, I was reminded of how the Beloved's beauty is an invitation to principle, freedom, sacrifice; a seduction intended to set us free. If that Evensong was undoubtedly a gratification of sensuous hankerings for years denied, it immediately plunged me into a state of mind not remotely akin to comfort, ease or uplift; but into something more like outrage and disgust.

Back in my room at the commune that evening, I was seized by self-loathing, almost overwhelmed by my worthlessness in light of that supreme worth I had just witnessed. It was all an absurd response to exaltation, I admit; but the insidious mental habits of a lifetime with depression do not die easily, if they really ever die at all. With dangerous ease, my mind began to be infested by thoughts of self-slaughter, the murder of this fixed, paralyzed creature I felt I was once again becoming. But then I recalled the Beloved; and gained enough realism to do one of the sanest things I had done for months.

———

Instead of killing myself, I killed my room, breaking every piece of furniture, tearing apart every book, smashing mirrors and lights until darkness and exhaustion stopped me. Upon awakening the next morning, I decided to abandon the cant-ridden rooming-house.

By early May, I was walking in the west-country of Ireland. If lonesome, I was at least an ocean away from the desperate, loathsome solidarity of the commune. For most of that season of slow drifting across the wildest districts of Ireland, I hitch-hiked or walked. My haunts were the crumbling tops of the towering sea-cliffs that wall in the west side of the Aran Islands, off Galway, their tall, rugged faces beaten by cold Atlantic gales, and then the boggy hills of Connemara. Above all other pleasures were hikes across the rocky, mist-swept mountain and sea-swept promontories of the Dingle Peninsula.

It was a time to give thought to the strong, strange forces that had caused my sudden, catastrophic breakdown, the frantic casting-away of my stuffy, formal clothes, the move to Toronto, the whole dizzying sequence of events from South Africa onward.

I found no answers in Ireland. Perhaps there are no answers to my questions. But I found a place that was, in its way, bread for my hunger. To this westernmost edge of Europe, fifteen hundred years ago, men and women had fled another dying world and its soul-withering technologies—warfare, forced starvation by enemies, military and cultural dominations, the paralyzing pleasures of luxury. On those storm-battered promontories, they had constructed the tiny beehive huts of stone that still stand, witnesses to the Beloved's Spirit and siren call—the one revolutionary spirit that leads, not to horror, but to liberation from the social madness of the day.

In these cold dwellings of the early Irish monks, hidden in the clefts of rocks high above the sea, I was recovering an ability to speak a language of the heart I had almost forgotten. I was slowly relearning to pray.

May, 1970

Ascension Thursday—as always, it seems, a Thursday of warm breezes and the green urgings under the ground, just making themselves known—

A curious festival in the Church's annual cycle, it's always struck me, but one I love: when the People of God commemorate the withdrawal of the Beloved from the world, his reception into the clouds. And two men, angels of glory, standing there (as St. Luke tells it), interrupting the pious calm with the words: Why are you staring at the sky? <u>Go back to the city</u>—

Now we await his return in the city, the pleroma when Jesus will be all, and all in all, returned to those who love him, the physical icon of the pierced, wounded and crucified God we shall never see, feel, again—

humanity is much given to clearing of fields, huge openings of forests, demolitions exceeding all that is necessary, the creation of flat, empty spaces of delusion, where we build our project of refusing to let go—

but the Beloved will return to little clearings in the forest, like light falling from heaven—clearings only large enough to allow us to see the sky a little—he will descend to unbuild, undo, be the quiet and absence and

> letting-go, *Gelassenheit, in the centre of renewed*
> *existence, the reforested world unworlded at last by*
> *the condescension of the divine into nothingness—*
> *the Cross—*
>
> *nothingness, absolute absence, at last revealed as*
> *compassion—*

My decision to move out of the wrecked, wretched room in the commune into an uptown apartment had probably been inevitable from the day I moved in with the communards. My next choice of residence had largely to do with what was available near the church I had attended on Easter, and to which I returned after Ireland.

One freedom had been attained; I was a Christian again, and would practise as one from that time onward. The freedoms of sexual intimacy, however, continued to elude me.

The opportunity for learning the languages of carnality was there: like any metropolis, Toronto is an easy place to find a night's companion—though my inexperience in sex made it hard for me to do even that. I did not know the codes, rites, the etiquette of sex (if that does not seem like too prim and antique a word for something so basic) that seemed familiar to everyone else my age in Toronto.

Then my friend Deborah turned up suddenly, and asked to stay with me. For a short while that autumn, I believed that sexual intimacy had come to me, gift and blessing, without my having to learn codes foreign and only half-comprehensible. What I did not know, or at least did not learn soon enough to keep from falling in love with her, was that the Toronto visit was merely a stop on her way to the American south-west, where she was eventually to join the man she really did want to be with. One foggy day in December, when I was away from the apartment, she received the call for which she had been waiting, packed, wrote me a note, and vanished.

I do not doubt that Deborah's disappearance had to do, in part, with my disabled, dispassionate receiving of pleasure—every depressive's secret sexual defect, I suspect, and nothing a sensuous woman like Deborah could sensibly be expected to put up with for long. But such sober insight into her departure came to me later, after the fading of ordinary rage and hurt. But when it did come, this reflection was not attended by any strategizing about how to find a replacement for what I had lost. Rather, it was accompanied by a certain relief, since I would no longer have to pretend I was enjoying sex, when what I really wanted was intimacy. And there was another outcome: a dawning curiosity (or emergence into half-light of long-repressed desire) about what such intimacy would be like with a man.

Reared by and around women, isolated from any sexual enactment by depression and my weird psychic projects of unpleasure, possessed of something akin to horror of sports, I knew almost nothing about men: how they talked and behaved, what their bodies looked and felt like, what physical intimacy with a man would be.

I soon found out. The sexual encounters and interludes I had with other men in the wake of Deborah's disappearance were fumbling affairs. I knew about the plumbing, mechanics and technical details of how several kinds of sex were done, but that very knowledge seemed to work on me like an anaesthetic when in bed with someone else. The sex was thus rarely pleasurable or interesting enough to make me want to go on with any particular game with the same person very many nights, and was apparently never of great interest to my partners.

Not that I regret those nights and days, the human closeness of them, even the funnily inept sex—and least of all do I regret the initiations into new sorts of intimacy. The nearness, just lying naked in the embrace of another man or woman, caressing and being caressed, was still strange to me—but it was *enough*, and deeply satisfying even when not accompanied by much energetic performance. It was during one of those placid evenings in my apartment that the man in my arms said he loved me. In my thirtieth year, I was hearing those words for the first time.

Like most curious grown-up men who find erotic closeness with other men attractive enough to venture it more than once—and have a baleful tendency to intellectualize everything—I wondered then, and from time to time thereafter, to what class of sexual mortals I belong. *Bisexuality*—a term I had not heard before—was coming into vogue around 1970.

I disliked the idea and term for several reasons. For one thing, it rang loud with high-school biology class connotations; it sounded like something one would say of a South American frog or a field crop, not a human being. If *being* bisexual were possible, then it would involve a sort of revolving infidelity I could not accept on moral grounds. And calling oneself *bisexual,* as people did, rather noisily, in those days and since, always struck me as faintly mendacious—a rather feckless attempt to conceal a preference for homosexual practice or the ignorance of bodily desire that comes from impotence or cowardice when it came to testing the waters until sure which waters one liked.

While firmly designated *male* at conception, the sexuality churning inside me since childhood has always been decidedly fluid and mischievous in its choice of objects, obdurately refusing to confine its business to either one or the other half of humankind. I consider this state of affairs one of several psychic snarls left tangled and unsorted after adolescence was done— during the time, that is, when the energy that should have been directed towards resolving sexual matters was being lavished on the all-consuming project of depression.

The social pressure to resolve the issue in adolescence would have been enormous, had I any friends then, or any contact beyond the most perfunctory with my peers. I would have been expected to choose what I would be—a choice that, in turn, meant decamping from ambiguity into this or that mutually exclusive pattern of society; dressing in this or that way, living in this or that neighbourhood of like-gendered people. It would have meant becoming something I was not, which was anything specific in the vocabulary of the sexual universe.

By the time I was twenty-nine, however, I had at least decided I liked sex with Deborah, and the prep-schoolish sex I had enjoyed with some men. Furthermore, I was coming to the conclusion that I did not want or really need to choose between abstract cultural options. I did want a companion. But where was I to find one?

Queer culture, the male gay response to oppression and, more recently, AIDS—aggressive, showoffish, impolite, egregiously individualistic—was nothing I wanted to be a part of; and anyway, it hardly existed, at least to my knowledge, in the early 1970s. What was ready to hand in Toronto was the quaintly sleazy homosexual culture of reigning queens and bars and styles of promiscuity, ranging from furtive to romping—a sphere of experience that offered me no place within its mesh of gestures and grandiosities.

What I could not bear was the society, the sociology, of homosexuality as I knew it then: the bars, the predatory prowling, the hustler scene on Yonge Street, the grimness and desperation of the gay sexual pursuit—all situations too much like depression, too similarly lacking in travesty, subversion, humour. But without entering the society, I discovered, there could be no easy enjoyment of the style. Throughout the increasingly militant, simplistic 1970s, the mere enjoyment of cultural slides and the ornate twists of perversity, marginality, Otherness, was not considered good enough by the homosexual elders and the newly Out. One could not luxuriate in the style of polysexuality without adopting a stance of militancy I could not adopt, doing what I could not honestly do—publicly running-up one's flag, "coming out," taking a side *for* and *against* a sexuality. Such gestures were considered *de rigueur* then, and seem even more important now.

Camp, however, was and remains an attraction, a delight, however obsolete. Since AIDS, almost everything in the culture of homosexuality has changed, and camp seems largely moribund; but twenty-five years ago, that antidote to the peculiar seriousness of mass society (hence depression) was much alive. I enjoyed it, if only from the distance, because it was everything depression was not: flamboyance, an absence of anger coupled with harmless transgression, a complex, glittering, hilariously insulting humour—"I don't have to *tell* you you're ugly, because you *know* you're ugly!"— almost incomprehensible to any man stitched inside the fabric of male mastery and male discourse. Here was perversion as aesthetics; and that *aesthetics*, the style, intrigued me in ways the gymnastics of perverse sex never has. (Long after my marriage, well into early middle age, I still wore rhinestone brooches and other such glittery things whenever I could get away with it, partly to be cheeky and contrary, but mostly because I loved the erotically ambiguous sparkle.)

When my brief spell of early sexual intimacies was done—this was still rather early in 1971—I had made a decision of sorts about what sexual route I would pursue. If my hateful depression would ever allow me any enduring companionship, I would find it either with a woman or with a celibate community of Christian men. I dreaded living alone, and resolved to do so no longer. I wanted a loving family, with the ballast and continuities I had never known, and I believed I could find that either with men joined in spiritual commitment, or in a more usual family, with wife and children.

In keeping with the pattern of quick moves and experiments I was making in those years of dawning identity—and contrary to the sensible thing to do, which was to keep on seeking where I happened to be—I decided in the spring of 1971 to buy a BMW 600 motorcycle and spend the summer on a large circuit of the United States, starting in the deep South, proceeding through Texas and the south-west, and coming back to Toronto via California and the coast and then the Canadian prairies—in search of a woman or an inclusive community, if not safe, then at least rich in the adventure of intimacy.

I did not find a community of men that would have me, or at least one I wished to join. To my surprise, undiminished to this day, I found a woman prepared to live with me forever.

---

28 March 1971

*March ends cold—a dry, waiting time, waiting for my
motorcycle to come, waiting for teaching to be done and
over—the edge of being is always like this, daybreak,
breakdown—*

27 April 1971

*April—time of rain squalls and brilliant lights breaking
through the scuttling clouds—
    tonight, riding my bike in the industrial zone so quiet
in midnight pooling darkness—tonight, and then
another night, and not so many nights until I pack the
bike and ride away from Toronto suicide night-thoughts,
discouragements failures of the year, over the world's edge
into mists, precarious unknowing—into what worlds
I do not know—yet even there is Christ, the ridgepole
in which every angle of the house is held—*

I had never owned a motorcycle, nor even ridden on one, when I bought the BMW. The dealer was surprised when I asked him how to turn it on. We were both surprised when I gently upped the gas flow and the motorcycle shot out of the parking lot across six lanes of traffic, ending up in the yard of a distressed neighbour of the bike shop, whose pansies I had annihilated before figuring out how to stop. It took me two days to get the

bike home from across town, what with wobbles and wrong
turns and finally a dead battery, another weekend of riding it to
decide this crazy thing was really what I wanted to do, and a
month to get my licence. I was off the day after that.

The adventures of my bike trip through America in the
summer of 1971 were never routine; some were deliciously
strange, others strange enough to make me want to forget them.
But one, I shall never be able to forget. It began in July of that
summer, after I had arrived in a New Mexico town one hot,
dusty afternoon, and stopped off at a soda shop in the university
district for a Coke. After slinging myself on to a stool at the
counter, dropping my helmet on the floor and ordering a drink,
I noticed that the man seated next to me was reading Simone
Weil's book *The Need for Roots*. No other book would have
drawn my attention with quite the urgency of this one. During
my first flight from graduate school, after I had been told to
withdraw from study and had done so, the Anglican priest who
had given me refuge also gave me Weil's book, in hope that its
rigorous counsel would help me. I did not read it at that time,
though the slow suffering in Weil's writing, her philosophic
hungers, were to become precious to me. Striking up a conversation with another reader of it seemed like a natural thing for a
lonesome biker, new in town, to do.

What happened next can be told almost as swiftly as it
occurred. Tony got me a roof to sleep on—in the American
south-western desert, flat roofs on adobe houses are *la moda*—
and, the next evening, introduced me to the woman who had
moved from Arkansas, her young daughter in tow, to be with
him. She and I, upon meeting, knew immediately where we were
headed. Margaret was looking for a fast way out of town, out of
a dreary, poor-paying teaching job in a shabby parochial school,
and out of proximity to Tony. She also wanted something better
for herself and her daughter than she had found in New Mexico,
among "the whole sick crew"—as she called her beer-drinking
friends, lifting a nice phrase from Thomas Pynchon's *V*.

As for my part, I was sure that anyone who got to know me would not want to marry me, so peculiar were my proclivities, interests and history. Any wedding would have to happen quickly, or not at all. And I had also decided that marriage was all I would settle for—not a trial period of living together, but the kind of relation that starts at a given moment before God and human witnesses in a public ceremony of the Church of Christ, and that would end only with the death of one of us. Before we were married, I told Margaret everything about myself I thought she should be warned about—my love of cats and dislike of dogs, the precariousness of my academic position (since I already knew I would not be finishing Ph.D. studies), the constitutional position of the monarchy in Canada, the sludgy Toronto winters, my devotion to Anglicanism, and, of course, the details of my sexual encounters, as limited in number, variety and interest as they surely had been, and the tale of my depressions and therapies. Remarkably, none of it deterred her.

And so it happened that, after three weeks of conversation, having decided to marry first and get to know each other later, Margaret Cannon and I were joined in holy matrimony by the faintly bewildered dean of the city's Episcopal cathedral. We set out at once on the trip back to Canada, with Margaret and her eight-year-old daughter and Abyssinian cat in the Volkswagen Beetle, me on my bike—a trip interrupted only by quick stops at the Louisiana and Arkansas homes of our families, who were stunned in disbelief.

Almost immediately upon our arrival in Toronto, and my resumption of teaching for the last year of my three-year appointment, I was told that the contract would not be renewed. The man who told me was also the man who had brought me up, thereby doing me the second of perhaps the two best things anyone had ever done: hiring me and bringing me to Toronto when I was still in the depths of intense mental disarray; and firing me, thereby forcing me to make a decision about what I would do with my life, instead of merely drifting aimlessly towards an academic career for which I was neither intellectually nor temperamentally suited. I was thirty, and without a clue as to which way to go.

———————

14 December 1971

> *the agony of this time, the wondering onward, i feel
> in my bones—restlessness of prairie fire, not knowing,
> flickering in the night across the expanse of dark-
> lightened dark—what is the voice I hear now? what is
> the pillar of fire, leading—where is it, and leading
> where, through what angles, tensions, turns, releases
> in the primal wave of it?—*

CHAPTER *5*

Homecoming, Slowly

F *rom* earliest childhood until my meeting and marrying Margaret, there had been no one who had
stayed in my life. Suddenly there was someone, two people in
fact, Margaret and her daughter Jacquelyn, sharing my apartment, table and life, and showing no signs of leaving. I did not
like it. It distracted me from habitual absorption with my symptoms. Life abruptly became practical in ways I had never experienced, a fabric of interchanges I had never known—furniture to
buy, a school to find for Jacquelyn, household chores and habits
to negotiate. And all this, with a woman and a child I hardly

107

knew, who were nevertheless suddenly closer to me than any two people in my life had ever been.

Somewhere deep in my mind, I believed this new domesticity would all come to an end, sooner or later; that after staying for a while in Toronto, being shown the sights and introduced to the city's culture, Margaret and Jacque would drift away, as everyone else had done. The recognition that this was not to be dawned on me one afternoon in the autumn of 1971, when, on one of our busy, ceaseless excursions about town, Margaret simply turned around and told me to stop treating her like a tourist. She wasn't going anywhere. This was, she calmly said, forever.

It was a piece of knowledge I took to uneasily. Not because I wanted to be alone again, nor away from Margaret—who was, after all, the first person to find in me some attraction so deep that even my oddities, feverish moods and changes, unpredictable ups and downs, did not deter her. But in some other conflicted, anxious zone of myself, I found myself wanting to undo it all, turn back time to some hour before we had met.

If my marriage was to become sustenance and strength, it was then still something approaching *menace*. For within Margaret, then as now, is a secret room without door or window, a secret life that I could not, cannot penetrate, with shelves stacked high with memories that are hers alone. To understand that such secrecy exists in others, and that it must be left unviolated forever, even in those with whom we enjoy the most intense intimacy, is to be civilized; to cherish this distance is to be in love. I had first experienced civilization in the curious instant of insight that came when the man in the plaid shirt crossed the street. I was learning to love in the midst of more difficult, slowly dawning insights, ones more vulnerable to darkening by depression because more intimate and harder to understand.

Love is depression's most potent enemy. Yet love cannot exterminate the disorder, or cure it—contrary to the delusion common among those who have fallen in love with depressives. If anything, the compassion of another person threatens the crouched demon of depression, inflames it and triggers its terrible whisperings. In the early months and years of my marriage, depression's cold voice never stopped telling me that my life sentence was to live alone—that marrying Margaret had put me in violation of parole, liable to punishment for exchanging the absolute certainties of depression for the ambiguities of life with a living, evolving woman.

The depressive malignancy always seeks to protect itself from exposure in exactly this fashion: by breathing into conscious mind the lying, paradoxical notion that more radical isolation, yet more intense doses of cruel purity and abstinence are the only ways to alleviate the symptoms we despise. Thus does depression hide the true location of its lair, in repeating endlessly the quite plausible proposition that staunch individualism and self-reliance are the root virtues from which we've allowed ourselves to drift.

It is easy for all of us, not just depressives, to forget that this proposition is the ideological grease of the mass-cultural machine we live within. Without continually fancying ourselves "independent" or "free," we would surely not be able to bear the monotonous day-to-day busywork, the stress of conformism, the levelling and subordination and time-wasting distraction that comprise everyday life in mass democracy. The torment of depression springs, at least in part, from the fact that we are independent, even if we don't want to be—dysfunctional, that is, within a culture that values smooth coordination and subjection to consumerism above all else, while ceaselessly broadcasting an entirely contradictory message about how we should behave.

For reasons partly physiological, partly temperamental and mostly unknowable, depressives react badly and sometimes obnoxiously to being caught in the pincers of this contradiction. The experience of intense isolation as a strategy of coping with the confusions of the world makes the depressive a true believer in individualism, that state of perfection always just beyond our grasp. Beyond all other persons, we are loyal to the discourse of "rights" and "personal liberties" that emerges from the propaganda of individualism. No one could believe more firmly than a depressive in the "right over one's body," the "inalienable power to choose," every notion embedded in the vocabulary of "emancipation"—without which self-slaughter, the end which the black dogs has in store for us, would be quite literally unthinkable.

Though not a prerequisite, depression may help some people see the fuzzy baffle of individualist ideology for what it is: a language that discourages our belonging anywhere. It also encourages the enmity to rootedness at the heart of depressive malignancy and the aversion to our only true human right: to be knit into the general communion of suffering, emerging and disappearing human presence.

We can become "individuals" in the modern sense, after all, only by ignoring the cries of the damaged world that can occasionally be heard through cracks in our smooth, liberal civilization. Answering that summons to mercy—the sparing of persons and ordinary beauties from reduction to raw material for the consumer market—could be a step towards liberty from individualism, hence, possibly, from depression. But that is perhaps only futile speculation. Chronic depressives are shackled so firmly by the language of self-hatred and worthlessness, our heads so full of the nattering of self-revulsion, that the potentially liberating call from the world's suffering heart can only rarely, if ever, be heard, and, if heard, more rarely answered. It is this selfishness that others see, and most despise, in us, and that grievous bond from which we desire most deeply to be free.

---

20 March 1972

Late wintry day, after walking in the woods near town...Buzzards, lacking magnetic needles in their heads to draw them to other summers, south of here, scrawl loops in the winter sky, eyes open for the dying, and then

the slow glide down on slopes of wind to feed—
   thank God for finitude, for the rub of the real
instant—otherwise my head would wander anywhere
today. The project: to drop all dreams, do the necessary
thing—
   but I spin outside the necessary things, scrawling
looping lines on the earth around me, nothing done—

The alternative I hit on immediately before meeting Margaret—a choice between marriage or monasticism—seemed paradoxical to me then, and afterwards. It would be years before I grasped their radical unity in indissoluble vows, unions profoundly unbreakable and mutual—the only remedies I could then imagine for the sickening drift of the anxious months and years before departing on the motorcycle trip that changed everything. The traditional rites of marriage are not, after all, very different from those of monastic obligation. Both insist on duty, loyalty, self-denial, the celebration of love and community—the surrender of orderly isolation and the acceptance of human communion, in all its untidiness.

Both marriage and celibacy, undertaken in the spirit of the stern, wise rites of the Church, are checks to self-possession, summons to personal sacrifices of ego that run counter to the heavy tide of selfishness in mass culture, hence to depression. But in 1971, if ready enough to make the public vows of marriage, I was not yet emotionally capable of changing the deadly egoistic habits of a depressed lifetime. No sooner had I married than the old struggle resumed, between love and the excision of myself from love. The result was corrosive indecision that quickly soaked into almost every corner of my soul—moral, sexual, emotional, intellectual. Afflicted by the notion that I did not know what to do, I did nothing—creating one of those passages of indecision and paradox debilitating to everyone, though especially so to those singled out by the black dogs.

It was from exactly this indecision that I had hoped marriage would rescue me. But I had only been married a few months when the black dogs returned, to weave their trap of hard magic and unreality. Many years of drawing feeble nourishment out of mass culture's barren ground had engraved deep habits. I wanted to get away from Margaret and Jacque, to make my way into the unknown future without them, because I knew no other way to confront it.

As the months after news of my dismissal from York University passed, I chose the easy sweetness of depression more readily than the hard bread of love. My indecision about how to proceed in my working life became addiction to comfortable torpor, self-pity, condescending pity of others. At the end of this downhill slope lies death—spiritual and moral certainly, sometimes physical. But the sensuously perverse pleasure of indecision, like that of lust, hides from its human object the death's-head at the bottom until it is too late to avoid sliding through its blind eyes into nothing.

July, 1972

Of the sickness of saying (of myself) these things: "on the brink," "I am seriously considering...," "I hope to...," when nothing happens, but the turning inside the gyre and maelstrom, where like all the flotsam and jetsam of the universe, I am always "on the brink...," "hoping to...," and going down.

of the putrefaction in me, rot in the soul's gizzard from the stirring of that talk: "on the brink," "going to..." and not doing it, only going around again the same turn—

nothing to do, nothing to be today, except what isn't there in the pictures I see, the advertisements. The deodorant ads tell me i stink, the underwear ads, bulging crotches, suggest I have no balls and cock to

fill the pouch, the books hoarded on my shelves
remind me of what i have not read, will not, cannot,
in the nothingness of nothing, and beyond that
nothing
    reading Cioran, <u>On a Winded Civilization</u>:
    "The man who belongs, organically belongs to a
civilization cannot identify the nature of the disease
which undermines it...Less restricted, the newcomer
examines it without calculation...As for remedies, he
neither possesses nor proposes them. Since he knows you
cannot treat destiny, he does not set himself up as a
healer in any case. His sole ambition: to keep abreast
of the Incurable."

As I eased towards deadly compliance with debility and drift—towards a kind of invalidism some people find perversely attractive—Margaret edged even faster towards disgust with what I was turning into, what I began to smell like. The break came one snowy morning late in 1972, when her mounting rage finally broke its dam, and came rushing at me like a tidal wave.

I do not remember exactly what was said, though I do remember very clearly the aftershocks. First, hurt—the normal neurotic resentment at having the game of worthlessness smashed by a thunderbolt of anger. (We are never angry at the genuinely worthless.) Then, revulsion at the thing Margaret's lightning flash had cast into abrupt, menacing relief: the wall I was building, brick by brick, around my body to protect me from the dangerous complicities of love, becoming, process, uncertainty. The summons Margaret issued was inescapable: a decision about the future, *our* future, had to be made.

On the last day of 1972, I sat down at the desk in my rarely used study—student habits, having a study among them, die hard—and wrote a list of career options, some more realistic than others for a man quite definitely over thirty. But even before I had finished jotting down the list, I knew which I would pick: "writer."

The immediate practical task, that New Year's Eve, was to decide what one must do to be a writer in Toronto, or anywhere. So I went on to make a list of resolutions.

Writers write, that was obvious. I resolved to write every day. And I did—even though I did not yet have a clue as to what I should be writing *about*—in every moment I could find, scribbling lines and "ideas" in notebooks, typing out my thoughts on whatever I happened to be reading, preserving what I believed to be sudden, wise perceptions on a portable tape recorder.

I resolved also to find the places writers were, to go there, and to meet them. Despite my good intentions, this resolution was not tardy in coming unstuck. I do not happily recall the innumerable, endlessly boring poetry and prose readings I attended in fulfilment of this resolution. Nor do I recall with any happiness my several early attempts to strike up purposeful conversations with men and women browsing in the literary sections of bookshops, only to discover that my gesture was almost always taken as a sexual come-on.

But the most important resolutions, as far as my future career was concerned, were to get my name in print quickly, to keep it there, and, when asked what I did, always to reply *write*, even though I had not yet made a penny from writing, and had no assurance that I ever would. Here, unquestionably, the word preceded the fact.

Curiously—or so it seems to me now, more than twenty years later—no qualification or description attached itself to this word *writer* that New Year's Eve, nor did I think to attach or try to locate one. The kind of writer I was to be was a matter of almost complete indifference to me. I have never felt the smouldering desire to be known as a great novelist, renowned poet, magisterial critic or shrewd public philosopher. The word *writer* simply lay on the page before me, empty of urgencies, specific programmes, even goals. It did, however, have an almost intoxicating aroma:

of being in the world in a certain new, resilient way, of turning from one manner of existence in language—marked by habitual, dark self-condemnation—towards another, as yet unknown. Stretching out beyond that word, that gate into larger life, was a vast undifferentiated plane, devoid of path or signpost.

———

January, 1973

> *"Many bear the wand, but few become Bacchoi..."*
> *(Plato, Phaedo 69c)*
> *:the work of the writer, the seeker, is beauty and*
> *rigour; ascesis of meaninglessness—we shall be*
> *meaningless, uninterpretable, and that will be the*
> *end, and all—*
> *an end to all rankling jealousies and hatred, all*
> *bitterness—against my past, my inadequacies, family,*
> *betrayers, the insulters, against all clamour and*
> *striving—and above all, the sense that I am not getting*
> *anywhere, tending towards no initiation, listening to*
> *the clocks inside my head, this wretched knifing into*
> *my heart—*
> *Christ Jesus, take my dance and make it moral, bless*
> *the tribe, the tribal in me, burn out of me all nostalgias*
> *for mysterium tremendum et fascinans—make me*
> *meaningless, bearer of wand in nakedness, Bacchus*
> *drunk on wine of daybreak, after whatever final*
> *morning the words are tending me towards—*

———

The question of what I was to write did not arise in those earliest days and weeks. But occasionally the question, why write at all, *did.*

Given my immediate intellectual background, that muttering inside my head was probably inevitable. The psychoanalytic notions adrift on the air in the seminar rooms of my graduate school, in the 1960s—Norman O. Brown was there, the teacher of us all—would have located the answers in the toilet bowl, or in what we deposit there, and how. In this popularized version of what Brown, in his famous book *Life Against Death: The Psychoanalytical Meaning of History*, called "the excremental vision," writing is shitting, a depositing of dirty marks on clean white pages. And, like excretion, it is also purification and liberation, an opening of mind analogous to the emptying of the body. The anus, open, becomes the body's eye for seeing the repressed, the dirty, what lies beneath.

It seemed natural to start with writing criticism—at least if *criticism* is understood, not as reviewing, but as an activity tinted with the medical connotations of its Greek etymology: a close scrutiny of feces and urine, spit and blood in order to determine the status and progress of the disease. If as a writer I've come to be almost exclusively concerned with the excretions of the cultural body—visual art and architecture, music and literature— my subject is, and always was, the sickness afflicting social being, the technological malaise, of which art is the principal symptom. Indeed, in the prelude of thought leading to this book, the particular ejectum of culture known as *depression* became the object of the same inquiry I've brought to many other topics over the years.

For if one central conviction controls this writing on an illness that affects millions, it is that depression is a culture like any other, knowable only in and through language and imagery— the distemper of a world, the spiritual and technological one we have made and inhabit, made visible in what we do, say and write and make. My job has been to read the traces, and see what they tell me.

Though I could not have known it at the time, the three-year period during which I taught was providing crucial practice in criticism of this sort. In addition to sustaining me intellectually during those first years in Toronto, my masters, Levine and Thompson, also provided me with models of the critical thinker, and with intellectual instruments for probing the body of contemporary culture.

Both professors—the phlegmatic Levine and the flamboyant Thompson—shared, and encouraged in me, an enduring skepticism about the twentieth-century mystique of technological mastery that brought the world insulin, but also Hiroshima; television and the Global Village, but also Auschwitz; the end of smallpox, but also the disinterested science that had produced the plague-culture in which the monstrous doctors of the Nazi death-camps worked, and Cold War psychiatrists carried out destructive experiments on minds of unwitting victims in the name of liberty and the American way of life.

For art—however more broadly I have come to define and understand it—should expose and resist the eroticized, soporific mass culture of words and images in which we swim, by which we are controlled, *by which we are depressed, oppressed.* The central danger in any cultural criticism lies in the ease with which one can fall for the thuggish allure of capitalist ideology, which will always be muscular, busy and colourful in a way the most rigorous thought never is. If I learned anything from the high-rolling 1980s, it was that any shotgun marriage of mass culture and high art is doomed to end only one way: with art the beaten wife, and pop culture the brutal, ever-forgiven, even heroized victimizer.

---

20 January 1973

*Went by Fifth Kingdom Bookshop today & there, what
I have been looking for—the little journals, poems and
writings, to fill with writing, mine—for me to be filled
by*

> *—and in it all, all of it the time in the book shop,*
> *terrific freedom, dispersing the ugly void-noises howling*
> *up out of the centre of the thing i am—the urgency is*
> *the yes to it all, the rush to play games of silence and*
> *words, silences we cross-stitch on the time we have, on*
> *the fabric of texts—*

———————

Were this autobiography, I could almost now tuck the tales of depression and its desolations into the trunk of baby blankets, toys, graduate-school papers and other memorabilia accumulated during the thirty-odd years before I became a writer. With a little lying, and many a quiet skip and sidewise slide, I could plausibly lay out the years of my life since January, 1973, as a smooth crescendo from confusion and obscurity to success and security in mass-media journalism.

Indeed, it's high time for a happy ending, or at least the famous "moment of truth" readers of biography wait for—the crisis in the struggle towards selfhood, the beginning of the lifelong effort to hold on to Truth and Success in the confusing thicket of untruth and dejection. In the scenario expected, the subject of the biography must remain, or most memorably fail to remain, true to the uniquely human project, the healing of self and society by the continually more aggressive prophylactic of *truth*, which alone can banish ever-encroaching error, untruth, unhealth.

Set out in bald outline, the time immediately after becoming a writer in early 1973 might seem like such a moment of truth.

Very soon after deciding to write, I found a commission to do my first published article, a study of the poems of Phyllis Webb for Frank Davey's literary magazine *Open Letter*. In the months and years to come, Davey's introduction of me to the writing world in his magazine, and to Victor Coleman and his literary circle at Toronto's Coach House Press, would bring me one opportunity after another to write, to publish, to see my by-line and thus know I existed as a writer. Among other key discoveries was the artists' group General Idea, on whose work I wrote my first extended consideration of visual art for *Open Letter*, and Toronto's small avant-garde art scene.

If depression had done anything good for me, it was to keep me clear of the more obvious lunacies of the drug and political undergrounds of the late 1960s. Its ill effect was to keep me distant from the most creative developments of this seethingly creative episode. As a result of both, I was a wide-eyed wanderer around the edges of Toronto's marginal artistic and literary culture in the early 1970s. Everything was new, nothing was uninteresting, all of it kept me writing—literary and art criticism for little magazines, a novel eventually published by Coach House Press, sheer linguistic experimentalism, literary essaying, translating. I became a fascinated reader of the literatures that flourished outside the ramparts of my graduate-school curriculum—the poetry and novels of the Beats and Robert Duncan, the fictions of Harry Matthews and Celine, Artaud and Genet, the thought of Sade, Heidegger and Nietzsche, the oracular texts of *I Ching* and the occult philosophy, and much else. For a while, I became so engrossed by the wisdom of *I Ching*, astrology, the Tarot, I considered becoming a diviner; but always, I had to acknowledge, divination was never for me the holy thing it can be, but only a way to create more texts, more pretexts for writing.

There was virtually nothing in writing, except for poetry, that I did not try during the seven *Wanderjahre* that passed between the New Year's Eve of my resolve to write and the utterly unexpected invitation, on a bitterly cold January day in 1980, to become art critic of Toronto's *The Globe and Mail*.

The turn towards writing on art in the 1970s cannot be separated easily from chronic depression; nor was it, nor would it ever be, a permanent transcendence of it. Indeed, for anyone both depressed and inclined to become cultural critic in the early 1970s, art provided almost perfect material.

Here was art that seemed tailor-made for the depressive: bookish, stringent, sanitary, detached. Those qualities much inclined me to write about it. I had been formed in a culture of books, had found what I would become in the matrix of language; and, to this day, can feel no comfort in a place from which books, learning, and the work of thinking have been excluded. My formative encounters with visual art were of a sort that invited more literary response than rapturous surrender. Indeed, I doubt that I would have become an art critic, or even been tempted to write about art, had the most significant art of those times not been so sternly indifferent to beauty; or had it not treated artistic beauty as mere sham and glamour.

―――――――

November, 1975

*"Like poison Miss General Idea, objet d'art, poised on
stiletto heels and bound in the latest fantasy, represents
a violent intrusion into the heart of culture....Myth
becomes reality, the seductress becomes the mother,
Miss General Idea gets a grant. Miss General Idea is
glamorous. She exists in a blissful perfection, ignorant
of dialectics. Miss General Idea has no misgivings,
no regrets, no political ambitions. Miss General Idea
is above all...a container wherein her followers
sense a great innocence." (Copied from GI text,
1975...*

*Putting on my best rhinestones for a night out on
the town—*

*i imagine myself a <u>critic</u> with the glam of Miss GI—
i dedicate my criticism to her, but it's <u>All About
Eve</u>, since i plan to snatch her crown.
what are my chances?*

―――――――

At the time I am writing this book, most of the ideals I cherished in my first years as an art critic—especially of the fluid relationship between art and criticism—have been blunted and turned into high style, earlier to my distress, now to my indifference. To visit museum rooms devoted to contemporary visual art everywhere nowadays is to be treated to expensive, complicated artworks disguised as antidotes to a culture saturated in sensuality, but themselves unbearably stylish. This slide of art into haughty piety, fashionable and lucrative uprightness or oddity or novelty has steadily diminished whatever joy I once found in contemporary art.

But if the anti-aesthetic was perhaps doomed to become *la moda,* I could hardly have come to art, perhaps even to writing, by any other route than an *anti-aesthetic* one. Among the most persistent symptoms of my depression had always been, and remains, an inability to enjoy a thing without a stab of consciousness, the menace of words. This is true, whether the pleasure is artistic or culinary, friendliness, erotic love, or mere sociability.

In our great-grandmothers' day, this annulment of the ability to experience pleasure was regarded as a mind disease, and given the charming name *anhedonia,* which sounds to me like a Victorian house plant. Nowadays, anhedonia is no longer considered a separate illness, but rather a disorder embedded in more general depression. It is perhaps just as well that I found a profession that demanded more understanding and intellectual penetration than enjoyment. Most people, I imagine, go through periods of mild to severe numbness of spirit, body, and emotion—after the death of a loved one, for example, or after the collapse of a marriage or a career, or during illness. This benign anhedonia—if such a thing could be called benign—does not last long. After a while, you get over it, and return to the old things that gave pleasure, or perhaps find new ones. Yet when wired into the general syndrome of depression, it can be quite bad enough in its own right to send people in search of psychiatric help, and is apparently the immediate reason many people make their first appointment with a psychiatrist.

Anhedonia was not the prompt of my first search for medical help—by that time I had passed beyond wondering why I felt so little pleasure and was grasping at bits of wreckage simply to keep from drowning in a sea of crippling symptoms. But it had been a problem for me all my life, and it still is, even when just mildly depressed, which is perpetually.

That having been said, much great art and architecture, contemporary or otherwise, has the power to slash through the soft, cottony baffle quilted around my mind, and let in pleasures so acute as to be almost painful. So does a peculiarly small range of music. I suspect I should not even know music was anything more than another item on the shelf of cultural commodities that cultivated persons were *supposed* to appreciate, had I not discovered, in 1983, *Parsifal,* and then, in quick succession, the other music dramas of Richard Wagner. Over the last decade, hardly a week has gone by—and, in winter, hardly a day—without my listening to another recording of a Wagner opera, or the same recording over again, the full orchestral and vocal score open on my lap.

The confinement of my interest in music almost exclusively to Wagner strikes my musical friends as strange, even comical, and occasionally perverse; for my wife and daughter, it is merely another burden to be borne. I do try to listen to other composers, though I invariably drift back into the orbit of the old tyrant of Bayreuth. But for whatever reasons, Wagner satisfies in me a hunger for delight, sensuous and intellectual, and provides a measure of that pleasure in being curious and alive that I take to be the normal lot of undepressed humanity.

Most of the time, I imagine, depressives merely *believe* that beauty is there, somewhere. We may be able to talk about it, as though we have felt it. If it is our job to do so, as it is mine, we can even write about it—the virtuoso use of paint or steel or plastic, the bright game of volumes and densities, the plays between the far and the near across the transaction of middle, human distance, the intriguing intellectual and cognitive strategies that have been at work in art since before recorded history.

But there will be no happy ending to this book, not here, not later. At least for the neurotic, to know the truth is not to be set free. Anyway, the people closest to me, my dearest friends and most knowledgeable colleagues, would recognize in any such ending less inspirational victory than pure duplicity. Though even if I could fool myself, and some readers, into believing that all's well, doing so would only confirm the most mischievous superstition about depression: that all its victim needs is a good job, an interesting career, a loving family, and all will be well.

All of us, and depressive writers perhaps most of all, wish to believe such nonsense. The depressed are continually, rightly furious that there is no cure, nor a wholly reliable palliative— not even in the offices of the best psychiatrists or in the most precious pharmaceutical concoctions. None of us wishes to believe the truth: that depression is the most obstinate experience this side of malignancy and death, a deadly presence in language and thought as inextricable as an inoperable tumour. Were I to lose my grasp on this fact, were my resignation to it to slip, I doubt if I could ever write another word.

---

11 April 1973

i wish to know precisely <u>why</u> the little body inside my
body has died,
   and <u>more important</u>
   why I have to keep its tiny mummified corpse clean
and fed and entertained—and why i am not allowed to
do something else but bring it food, argue with it, keep
the little dead body inside me amused, which being dead
has no eyes to see, no ears to hear—
   —there is no end to it, there is no end of therapy—the

*little mummy will be there, and will be there and will,
and that is true, the never-ending of it—today the dark
inside its burial shrine my body is very dark, deep,
reeking of filth and slow decaying body and I must keep
the little rotting body in me amused by what i do—and
people in the world see me and are amused by me, but is
the little body? how can i tell for its expressionless face?*

*Pericault, <u>Mémoires historiques sur la Louisiane</u>, on
the Biloxi of New France:*

*"After mummifying their chief by smoking him over a
fire, they set him up on his feet along with other chiefs
in a 'temple.'" His family visit him from time to time.
"Some ask him why he has allowed himself to die before
them...If there had been some fault in his government
they take time to reproach him with it. However, they
always end their speech by telling him not to be angry
with them, to eat well, and they will always take good
care of him."*

*a tribe of neurotics. i would have felt at home there.
Thunder, the Biloxi hero, becomes sick and finds
liberation. i would have felt at home among the Biloxi,
at home in their illusions, and in their fate, to be a
language that disappears*

(Thunder has an uncle named Taunt.)

A great deal of money is being made off kindly, instructive books, implying the possibility of reversing anhedonia, and finding the pleasure that eludes depression's sufferers. As I have suggested in this chapter, a certain way of negotiating one's way through and around depression is possible; but that is all.

Chronic depressives and the merely discontent will refuse to believe me. A fellow-journalist, an expert observer of the international book-publishing business, told me I should call this book *Sixty Days to a New You*. She had no doubt that, with that handle, hefty, quick sales would surely follow—simply because the market is insatiably hungry for any new book with such a title, to replace all the books with similar titles that have failed to make a change in anyone's life.

But how do we account for this hunger? It is, I think, because most of us dwellers in liberal, secular democracy are crude Darwinians at heart—credulous believers in the inevitable ascent of all humanity, and the recapitulation of phylogeny in each human soul, from a state of dumb, brute violence to gentility. Unless, of course, the process is thwarted. If it always *is* thwarted, if we find ourselves stalled in our evolution from muddle to clarity, victimhood to mastery, then, says the little Darwinian within, we must seek out the force thwarting our ascent, and overcome it. The racist turns against the Jew or black, the anarchist turns against the institutions of state and society, the totalitarian against disorder—and the depressive, who is at once racist, anarchist and totalitarian, turns against himself.

Indeed, no population in the contemporary bourgeois world is more intensely, predictably Darwinian than the chronically depressed, and within that population, the writers and artists are perhaps the most Darwinian of all. We hate ourselves, sometimes to the point of unleashing violence against ourselves, for our mysterious inability to be on time for the evolutionary flight to the glorious future. Like most other people, we have become nearly unshakable believers in the liberal hopefulness that says we can make the flight if we just try hard enough, if we somehow learn how to get there. Perhaps the best any of us can hope to achieve during psychotherapy is a measure of distance from our obsessively demanding Darwinism, and the erasure of the obstinate optimism we writers, makers, artists have so much trouble letting go of.

CHAPTER 6

In Writing

A *writer's* journal is a shed for timber and bricks, stored up for the future. It is a place to keep the materials from which poems will be raised, novels built, criticism crafted. I had made diaries of that sort for years before definitely hitting on writing as a profession: collecting my jottings on bound pages in blank books ruled or plain, and on thousands of loose papers typed or handwritten and stacked in folders, on the backs of envelopes, boarding passes, the fly-leaves at the backs of books. This baggage always accompanied me into every study I've inhabited, shelved within easy reach.

But in all my journals—barns piled high with ideas, phrases, provocations harvested from hundreds of books—has always been a taint, the faint odour of depression's peculiar seepage and drizzle.

For that reason, I suppose, in the course of writing this book, I have found it both necessary and almost unbearable to look at the journals I've kept so long—since they recall the prodigious energies I have wasted on noting every trouble, however slight or banal, on commemorating carefully the passing of shadowed feelings as though they were new or important. The journals are reminders of an enthralment with the supreme folly of depression: the lazy pleasure it gives when we dignify its repetitious drivel in writing, our complicity with this peculiar condition of language, mind, culture by giving its whinings the status of discourse.

Though in 1964 I did not yet have the words for it, I had encountered the "neutral power, formless, without a destiny," as the French author Maurice Blanchot has called it, "which lies behind everything that is written..." *neutral* in the sense in which beasts or earthquakes are neutral, devoid of conscience or dread.

The keeping of a journal, Blanchot tells us, is ostensibly an understandable thing for a writer or would-be writer to do, inasmuch as it provides an alternative to some more active aversion to formlessness. It creates "a Memorial" to the self steadily vanishing into the act of writing. The unrolling text provides "a series of reference points that a writer establishes as a way of recognizing himself, when he anticipates the dangerous metamorphosis he is vulnerable to..."

At the same time, the Journal, as genre, is a symptom. The keeping of one tells those whose understanding can penetrate the text's skin that the keeper "is no longer capable of belonging to time through ordinary firmness of action, through the community created by work, by profession, through the simplicity of intimate speech, the force of thoughtlessness."

Now that I have gone through those thousands of leaves, I am left with the conclusion that they are worthless. And yet only what has had worth, and lost it, can be truly worthless. Their value consisted principally in the pretext, the excuse they provided for writing down things as a way of forgetting them. Perhaps the cherishing of these unread volumes and sheaves of paper through many years, through many changes of city and home, springs from a superstition that, should I crack the dry, dusty boxes in which they have been stored, the purged, hidden ideas and words would come flying back to me, throwing my mind back into the very conditions of emotional disjuncture under which most of the entries, until recently, were written.

On the rare occasion I have been asked why I do this, my politely insolent explanation for jotting down the happenings of each day is that it is an inherited trait, like baldness.

———————

It entered the genetic trace of Mays men and women, as far as I can tell, towards the end of the last century. There are no diaries until the generation after that of my great-grandfather, John Matthew Mays, an impoverished ex-rebel from South Carolina who moved to Texas and made himself wealthy there as a banker and merchant. The diarizing begins, perhaps significantly, not with this man—too busy with war, displacement, rebuilding and other discontents of modernity to do much writing—but in the generation of his children, or of some of them. One who did *not* keep diaries, significantly, was Helen Mays, last-born of Captain Mays's children, and much like her father. She was a person of acts, not fantasies: she escaped east Texas early, studied at Columbia University in New York, then went to the fledgling Soviet Union, where she worked tirelessly for children orphaned by the post-revolutionary civil war. Her letters and cards, postmarked Moscow, are factual accounts of suffering and success— the sorts of things her father would have written, I imagine, had he written at all.

The men and their wives were another story. Disinclined, for the most part, to work hard at creating new wealth, the sons of

John Matthew Mays who survived into adulthood drifted past wildly pointless teen years into lives imitative of their seamlessly genteel, autocratic banker-father's, yet always playing the game a little beyond their means—at the social station to which their birth entitled them, but which their diminishing wealth could not sustain.

It is in this gracious, undriven generation, born into the philistine, optimistic prosperity that came to America after the Civil War, and into a *fin-de-siècle* sensibility sensuous and unreal even in east Texas, that the writings start. There are volumes of them, beginning with my paternal grandmother's quotidian notations, from about 1890 onwards, all to do with who came to call and when, who died and how, the carry-on around her marriage in 1904 to John Matthew Mays, my grandfather, and the subsequent childbirths, what time the train departed for San Antonio and the condition of the hotel in which she lodged when visiting relatives there, the baleful effects of humidity on nerves and joints at home in Louisiana, and the tonic effect of the climate at the family's wintering spot in the Rio Grande valley.

These diaries add up to almost nothing. They are an accounting of teas in the rose garden and Missionary Society meetings, deaths and births all taken in stride, in a spirit of encoded, enforced normalcy. There is piety in these journals, but each feeling and event is atomized in the writing by a single, peculiarly modern action: an endless listing. Narrative coherence—the sense that life is going somewhere—is absent. Nothing comes to a point. The writing remains so many fragments of text, floating on the still surface of a pool outside time.

My grandmother's daughter, Vandalia, took up the task of diarizing in this way around 1920. Vandalia's notations of each slight movement or realignment of power in her social world, of medical symptoms and remedies, and of copied Bible verses continued to within a month of her death in 1991. Like my grandmother's diaries, Aunt Vandalia's now seem to be performances of dread, a stalling of death, a postponement of thinking that one is ever tending towards it. The diaries seem to have been an attempt to ground herself, if on no more solid ground than the shifting site of writing.

By the time she died, my aunt's world was gone. The village in which she had once been a highly marriageable aristocrat, then a married duchess second only in social prestige to her mother, had been emptied of the people she had known. The customary social web had been swept away, the old people displaced by young suburbanites who knew nothing of my family, who remembered nothing of the fancy-dress parties and flirtations under the magnolias so dutifully noted in Aunt Vandalia's diaries. In the end, my aunt was reduced to listing the symptoms of her impending death, taking notice of the pain that afflicted the only citadel time had not yet taken from her.

My deceased relatives' diaries are reactions, as are perhaps all modern unliterary diaries, to the fearful changes in a world increasingly incomprehensible. Listing, after all, is one way to reduce the jumble of incomprehensible events into a set of manageable commodities, stacked on the shelves of journal-pages. The listing takes its place in the new America dominated by the product, and the having of products (or memberships, social events, "occasions"). In that sense, the listing in diaries is continuous with the mercantile, middle-class culture that, from the Civil War onward, was the public stance and code of the Mays family: an imitation in language of shelf-stacking, of luxury production for its own sake.

At the same time, my family's early diarizing emerges as an attempt to halt the rapid change characteristic of the culture they were written within. The principal topic of the records is the day-to-day performance of the rites required by gentility and piety—a routine unchanging from year to year, a maintenance of one's status in the face of social shifting and dislocation. While the undepressed may keep diaries and photo albums for other reasons I cannot now imagine, the pictorial and textual archive of a family constitutes, almost inevitably, a complex defensive lie.

Or—to put the matter in a more kindly fashion—it is a fiction, created by many hands and over many generations, to keep at bay a sense of decline, the encroaching reality of death, by deep-freezing every ephemeral happening in a book. The erosion of the solid and sure is countered by the suffocating intimacy of details, and the levelling flatness of fact piled upon fact. These are the qualities that make the diaries of my grandmother and my aunt both nearly unreadable and entirely *modern.*

---

8 October 1973

"time is suspended" in modern experience only when
we are immobilized by bodily process: temporarily
(in the moments the stool is passing through the anus),
permanently (in death.) Warner Münsterberger, "Some
Elements of Creativity Among Primitive Peoples:" the
origin of art lies in the worship and fear of the dead;
the immobilized; the body at the moment of ejection
from life, turd cast from the body of the world.
*   Art, culture—perhaps language itself—thus*
emblematic of "time suspended"—the museum, shrine
of objects "in time suspended," emblematic of the place
of evacuation—anus voiding dead turds, voice voiding
dead words, the world—round indeed—the bright
muscular ring we push through into the dead zone,
dung heap, dead heap, site of refusal and ejection,
beyond time, outside speech at last.

All the stories are there, in the diaries: tales of immorality, sexual infidelity, the stuff of almost anybody's biography.

In the culture of the plantation South—as in any strictly traditional culture—that state of annoyed subjectivity known as *guilt* plays no practical part in human affairs. A sexual escapade is almost always a fleeting matter, alleviated by a prayer, or by the conclusion that no one is going to find out what you did. If one does happen to be afflicted by sexual guilt, the symptoms are usually interpreted as madness, and the issue becomes medical. Guilty feeling, where I come from, is considered abnormal, and not easily tolerated among knowledgeable people.

Shame, on the other hand, is a matter altogether more serious. To commit a sexual peccadillo is to bring disgrace upon oneself, and especially upon one's family; it is among the most terrible sins. And yet the deed only becomes sinful when it produces that public embarrassment known as shame. Hence, in the traditional Southern culture of my background, there is no blame in sexual slippage, no hypocrisy in seeing one's lover on Saturday night and going to church with the family on Sunday morning, so long as it brings no shame upon those one cares for and is responsible for.

As it happens, no amount of rationalization or justification would prove capable of alleviating the profound guilt and shame I experienced when, in 1974, I succumbed to the forces of temptation and immorality.

My adulterous affair began with an erotic infatuation with a shy, handsome man, who shared a blossoming curiosity about me. This mutual interest quickly went the usual route—from playful attention, to affection, to bed. The affair was murderously high in anxiety, notably short on sensuous enjoyment and brief. It packed stultifying stress into me about my troublesomely unresolved sexuality, and the treason I had committed against my still-recent marriage. The relationship ended, partly because I could no longer bear the anxiety and partly because I could not bear the thought of the ruination of a valuable marriage by a relationship that would shortly, I was sure, mean nothing to me.

———

Weakened and made wretched by the telephone call that ended the affair, I was especially vulnerable to the coming of the black dogs, and, indeed, they did come that night.

The dogs did their business quicker than usual, as I recall. First, as always, came the desolation of spirit, the self-hatred and self-blaming. Then, abruptly, they stopped worrying my flesh and spirit, and began to weave round me the spell of their weird peace. Into that circle of peace began to come sweet thoughts of death, the real strategizing of self-destruction without any imagination of the suffering my suicide would bring to others or to myself. The kindliness of that moment was wonderful, intoxicating in its calmness, and no fear or doubt entered my mind as I patiently went about preparing the tools and means of my murder.

But somewhere in the spiritual world, out of earshot and beyond the circle of what I could see or sense as I quietly went about killing myself, battle was waged between the packs of hounds who haunt the darkness. Again, that night, the dogs of heaven won, and in an instant I remember as unspeakably painful—blinding light suddenly blazing into the sweet suicidal twilight—the heaven-hounds grasped me in their terrible jaws and dragged me away from the instruments of destruction. How I arrived there, I am not sure; but the next place I clearly remember is the emergency ward of the nearby hospital, where I was put on a rolling bed and transported to a room at the top of the building. The room had one window, covered with heavy wire mesh.

The next morning, Dr. Rosen, a non-resident psychiatrist about my age, made the rounds of the hospital's psychiatric floor. The situation was almost identical to the one in which I had found myself with David, five years before. I told Dr. Rosen my tale of woe, of self-hatred and my deserving to die, of my endless mistakes in love, in life, in career. He listened patiently for a few moments—I really did think, for a fugitive instant, I had found another David—until, without changing the expression on his face, said he found me obnoxious, and my heaving bosom and blinked-back tears boringly theatrical to boot.

If Dr. Rosen was disgusted by me, I was furious at him— which, by the very peculiar canons of psychotherapy, is almost always a sign of love at first sight. It was the beginning of a clinical relationship that has continued, off and on, for twenty years, and, I suspect, will go on until he retires or one of us dies or becomes permanently bored. (We have occasionally become so tired of each other that one of us has broken off the regimen of psychotherapy; but the breaks have never lasted very long, and I am soon back in his office, complaining about the usual things. Each time I have returned, by the way, Dr. Rosen has met me at his office door with a certain smile I have come to deplore, and the maddening words: "Welcome home!")

Dr. Rosen has not cured me; nor does either of us believe he can. Like my wife, however, he has always told me the truth as he understood it, and never pretended to know what he did not know. He has thereby helped me into a practice of living with depression without the lies to others and the self-deceptions that only compound the disorder's symptoms. Too, while his tongue can be very sharp, it is no sharper than the teeth of the hounds of heaven, and considerably more reasonable than they are. Largely due to his sharp tongue and often painful candour, I remain in warm and intimate relationship with the woman I married, her hair-trigger temper and rock-hard common sense as quick and tough as the day we met a quarter-century ago.

If I do not understand as much about sex as other men do, or seem to—what sexological category I belong in, for example, given the ready quickening of erotic feelings in me both for certain women and for certain men—then so be it. No man who goes through puberty dismally depressed and friendless, and puts off having sex until twenty-seven, thereafter having only a limited array of sexual partners, can reasonably expect to be Dr. Ruth.

---

10 October 1973

Daphne Marlatt read her poetry at A Space this week,
long lines—long lines, to possess the page, to possess

*the world. Her beauty is written on her by "happy
accidents," as she calls them...*

*   And of all her poems, the loveliest are her
representations of British Columbia sites, herded from
the unutterable into Being's field by the gentle tending
crook of language, wielded by the poet, whom Heidegger
calls "the shepherd of Being"—yet I should love to love
Daphne's work better than I do, since something about
what she does, this documenting of places, always rings
a wrong note in my head—how is this romantic project,
this getting-it-down before it disappears, these acts of
patient recording, something other than archaeology,
worship of the dead, tomb-robbing?*

———————

Whatever assembling and disassembling took place in my inner life, the script I cobbled together and tried to follow in the decade or so after 1973 was a patchwork filched from experiences new and old. There were sexualities criss-crossing, infidelities that never made sense, further religious meditations and stern recommitments, fallings-away from the vision of the Beloved again, then back into a draining drift of will. Off and on, too, throughout the 1970s and '80s were various courses of psychotherapy with Dr. Rosen—who has never found me anything *other* than obnoxious, hence an interesting patient—and the tempestuous love and struggle of being in a family, being married. Always, however, there has been the writing, taking me with it as it surged ahead of me, always beyond where I thought I wanted to go, or should be going.

I cannot speak of these decades without recollecting the thoughts of suicide, the despairs and periods of self-hatred, that recurred as the years passed—the abrupt dooms and gradual lightenings that came and went, as they always had, and probably always will. Much went on in the world lying beyond the peculiar ambit of my tiny illness—good and bad moments in work, in marriage, in health of which I could write much, were this a standard autobiography. But this book is another kind of tale, a sort of truthful fiction spun from discoloured, twisted threads pulled from the basket at the bottom of my soul, a fabric without hem or end.

In that curious stack of biographical fact that is my life, I find little to lament. To invoke the line from Sartre I earlier said I *wanted* to believe: my biography has indeed improved since the 1960s. I am saddened only by the recollection of the deaths of loved relatives and a dear and loyal friend.

For the inner truth and life of the biographical bundle others call by my name was to remain, after 1973 or so, much the same—undistinguished by anything that might make it "special," continuing to be typified by the same chronic symptoms afflicting any other depressed person, I imagine, anywhere. It is life lived in the semi-dark of the unwalled institution I dwell within, an institution constructed by doctors, theorists and other cultural enforcers long dead, whose legacy to us is self-recognition in the muttering of self-hatred.

It is a muttering that feeds off mass culture. We—all of us, depressed and undepressed alike—are continually being asked by advertising and colloquial expectation to be disgusted by what we are, what we have, how we smell, the options we have. Were we satisfied, there would be no buying or selling of powers and techniques of mastery, and of status commodities—no economy powered by desire, the tantalizing dream of complete fulfilment, no spiralling sense of lack among those who seem to lack nothing. The depressive is, in a certain sense, no different from any other mass-democratic citizen obsessed with lack, directed towards the filling of the bottomless pit in the inner place the soul once occupied, when people believed in souls. The depressed, however, cannot even be provisionally satisfied; hence the incessant whining that characterizes neurosis.

In going on with this story—one *not quite true*, in the sense the unsick use the word *true*—will I be believed if I say that very

little happened? Or at least very little—save one thing, the end of
my alcoholism—that can actually be called *new*?

———————

17 February 1980

writing something early Sunday morning, 2 a.m.
I guess—after drinking all evening in the hot Cabana
Room, got crazy with Queen Street people I knew
before The Globe *came to get me, and they were*
strolling by, dancing different now, getting into my
craziness and dancing, but differently now—lights
and beer and people, so different now, a week into
the job as art critic, *and after hours of drinking*
crazy in the Cabana Room with people all so different
now—
   crazy time of it, the lights a fun blur, slow lines in
the smoky air, punk band
   —the normal paranoia, the normal fright still there,
even in the odd slow smear of spotlights on the band,
making blue and red flashes through the glass of pale
beer, and a crazy time and I was crazy drinking and
everything is different—
   …maybe 10 a.m., not sure—Sunday, anyway—
hungover, headaches, the works—stupid to get
philosophical now—the dark side that slopped down
in the water last night is up again, visible, all ugly
with barnacles and weeds and things out of the past—
acid beer puke in the toilet: that's it and that's me,
mind in the toilet, puke down and flush and an
ending to it all—

———————

Journalism is attractive to depressives for the same reason writing diaries is: because it does not require the intimacy or the good-fellowship required by many other activities. Journalism insists on keeping definite distances, on being *in*, but not *of*, the realm of activity one is assigned to cover.

Hard questions must be asked, and answered—a process that one can carry on creditably, even when deeply depressed. And yet to answer such questions obviously involves leaving the shelter of one's study. To answer them regularly and publicly, as I have had to do since 1980, entails much social fusion with the world at large. So it was, in the early 1980s, with my visibility as a writer suddenly rising, that alcohol became the lubricant that made participation possible.

It may also have been the reason I fell into a pattern of fits and starts in psychotherapy, and finally stopped altogether. For alcohol usefully masked the obvious symptoms of depression that most grievously beset me—the shapeless gaze, the unfocused, slow movement of the body, the dead pallor. I drank for that reason, to quell the anxiety that would surge over me during even the least threatening social occasions. I drank to give my dread and hostility the appearance of geniality. I drank heavily to license sexual infidelities with men and women that would not have occurred had I allowed myself to remain in a state of normal moral consciousness. I drank to fend off depression. Finally, and then exclusively, I drank merely to drink, to be drunk—a state, despite its squalor and embarrassments, that was increasingly preferable to depression.

I was unfortunately protected in this insidious strategy of self-destruction by the mythic reputation of critics as brooding isolates and tipplers, a renown surely with a basis in both fact and popular mythology. The fact is that both talented depressives and talented alcoholics are certainly drawn, in outsized numbers, to occupations in which moment-by-moment accountability is limited to a degree unusual in private industry. I have found work as an art critic for *The Globe and Mail* a near-perfect way to earn a decent wage while tied down, unpredictably, from time to time by seizures of will, and collapses of competence that would make many other interesting jobs difficult, even impossible. There is never any shortage of reasons why a critic must be away from the office for days on end—exhibitions to see, studios to visit, museums and galleries outside town to attend. And advances in information technology over the last decade or so—especially the introduction of affordable home computers and telecommunications devices—have further weakened the already tenuous link between critic and desk, between writer and editor.

Nowadays, no boss need know when most of a writer's day was spent crying for no apparent reason, or sitting in a chair staring stupidly into space, or quietly drinking bourbon to numb the groundless ache—if the depressed writer is able to marshal his shrunken vitality and muddled thoughts to hit the deadline more or less on time with a readable story filed over a telephone line.

By the time I quit drinking, booze had not yet caused me to commit a firing offence. And to give the devil his due, it had given me the calm necessary to get through professional encounters that, otherwise, I could have endured only by a combination of brute self-repression, a dangerous crushing down of anxiety within me. Genial drunkenness saw me through openings at private galleries and public museums, the brief art-world whirls that regularly precede grand international shows such as the Venice Biennale, dinners with artists and dealers.

My drunkenness would have probably gone on being forgiven forever, as it had been forgiven by the art world since my emergence within it. There came a day, however, when I could no longer forgive myself.

———

28 December 1985

*the Feast of Holy Innocents, deep winter and quiet day,
in the country alone, peace after too much Christmas*

stuffing and doing, drinking and getting drunk every
day—
   —writing after a hung-over drive through white hills,
glittering and profound violet shadows cast behind hills
and trees, pure winter, Plato's archetype of it, come very
near the earth, in snow squalls and the dark brightness
of snow, even under the winter moons
   —and haunted by the hurt that never goes away, after
years of what the world would call "doing better"—i.e.,
the writing job, being in the world, known, all outside
me, there, the grasp on what I wanted when I decided
to be a writer
   —and the hateful dead man inside me
   hunted by hungry dogs
   haunted by them, hungering, unless blind drunk,
stupefied, then unfeeling them pacing in bright darkness
of winter suns and moons—then comes the sight of
snowdrifts and ice heaps by wind-tormented lake,
and the thought coming—of resting on one, of gazing
at winter lights of sun or moon on mist-tatters and
wind-torn scraps of cloud, until I slept and slept,
then did not sleep
   —ending weariness, ending drunk days and nights
and the ceaseless lying, ending the sensual, trite thing
inside me, its duties undone, but zero under winter
moon, white, virgin—

Since the morning of 29 December 1985, I have been drunk
only once. For a while, I allowed myself a taste of champagne at
a wedding, birthday or other festive occasion. In the last few
years, I have not done even that.

   I was not particularly headachy, bilious or otherwise hung

over that December morning, though I had spent the evening indulging in fine food and conversation, and much heavy drinking, at a friend's country home. And even if I had drunk enough the night before to give me the usual pains of a chronic alcoholic's daily morning-tide, I would not have quit for that reason. By late 1985, hangovers had become a way of life, to be endured until the first drink of the next day chased away the dreariness of the last one. Alcohol had never failed me, always smothering depression, distancing the menace crouching in dark corners, relieving the less odd troubles that shadow every life now and again.

On many occasions before the end of 1985, especially after a round of particularly heavy drinking, I had looked down the road and seen clearly where my liquid ally was leading me: the ruin of everything I loved. I saw the impending destruction of my marriage, the misery of my toddler, heartbreak for everyone who loved me, and the eventual annihilation of a successful public career to which I had come late, after many wrong turns. I could certainly not claim ignorance of the wreckage and degradation to which alcohol remorselessly leads.

Not even wretched memories had stopped me—not those of my maternal grandfather, naked and besotted, nor those of my father's cruelty and his wasted life. In some secret place inside me, so secret I could not then look at it, I perhaps still longed to be one with my alcoholic father, whom drink first ruined, then, in indirect fashion, killed. None of it had slowed down my drinking even slightly, or quelled my craving for oblivion. In alcoholic stupor I had found one condition—easily induced, infinitely indulged by others, never brought to reproach, concealable (or so I imagined)—preferable to the seething anxieties.

But whatever motives were at work, they abruptly receded that brilliantly clear December morning. Immediately after putting alcohol out of my life—hence ending whatever control over my moods it had given me—I began to rediscover that even the most artful dodger of depression, stripped of an old, trusty

defence, cannot avoid running into the truth of disorder at all
sorts of awkward, inconvenient times. The fateful moment may
be a deadline missed, a party inexcusably avoided, a pleasant
gathering of friends skipped, without explanation, merely to stay
home, secluded in my study. Or the cancellation of an important appointment with an artist or art-world intellectual at the
last minute, because I was no longer sure I could keep my hands
from shaking during the interview, or hold down the onset of
quiet weeping that is the depressive professional's equivalent of
a soup blotch on an expensive new tie.

Why I quit *that* morning, and not earlier, later, or not at all, I
do not know—though I have always had a hunch that calendar
date had something to do with it.

The twenty-ninth day of December is the anniversary of
Archbishop Thomas à Becket's assassination in Canterbury
Cathedral—or, in the vocabulary of the Church, his birthday
into new and everlasting life. He had become the leading prelate
in the Church of England, after all, because his king and friend
thought him a weak touch, an amiable drinker and man of pleasure who would go along with anything the king wished to do.
Thomas's appointment, however, had an astonishing effect on
the king's choice: it galvanized this happy, promiscuous courtier's
conscience, made him see the larger picture of his corrupt
society, put steel in his soul. Recollecting the life and death of
St. Thomas has been putting steel in the souls of untold numbers of pilgrims to Canterbury for centuries.

I had been moved to my foundations during a visit to the
spot in the cathedral where St. Thomas was struck down. Since
that year no twenty-ninth day of December had passed without
a recollection of this extraordinary man, his example of rigorous,
principled thought and action, and his faithfulness unto death. If
the feast-day of St. Thomas's martyrdom is rarely, if ever,
observed publicly by the Church—it comes too soon after the

exhausting liturgies and activities of Christmas—the festival occasioned a certain passing peace, a permanent thankfulness within me, when it came round again in 1985.

I write of this episode with no self-satisfaction, no sense of triumph about stopping. It cannot be attributed to "will-power," whatever that may be. Nor can I write frankly of it without some declaration of regret: for within me, living and dangerous and sweet, still lies coiled the impulse towards self-destruction and self-delusion that turned me into the alcoholic I was and am, and the drinker I could easily become again. The lust for descent into temporary oblivion has never left me.

If truth be known, I would never have allowed that unseen dove to penetrate my soul, sweeping away my determination to wreck myself with alcohol, had I the slightest idea of what new dark hells of depression and self-hatred my abandonment of alcohol would bring.

———

18 April 1986

*only two days of work on the book this week—unable to
sleep, this happening and that happening, and all of it
dragging me down, away from the writing—*
    *feel it is all falling apart, what i had promised to
make of these years of writing up art shows, this book
of the project, the going-on and doing it—i read, and
the words soak through me and away—i write, and the
tiny marks, these letters, pile up into nothing, drifts of
sand, wind-driven from whatever shape I heap them
into—*

2 May 1986

*too soul-sick to type
    no adequacy in me for the job, too stupid, ignorant*

no sleep for days—in odd minutes of half-sleep,
imagined doctors medicalizing me, down it
thing

———————

Kicking the bottle out of my life was obviously the right thing to do, though I now see how wrongly I went about it. I just quit. No Alcoholics Anonymous, no counselling, and, most seriously, no return to psychotherapy with Dr. Rosen—with results a more sensible person could have predicted. Alcohol is a sort of ramshackle, temporary defence against complete anaesthesia, and the coming of the black dogs. I was now wholly without defence.

The first long, humiliating defeat by this more virulent, more muscular post-alcoholic form of depression occurred in early 1986, during an eight-month leave of absence from the newspaper. My goal was to write a critical book on Toronto art, an inquiry and summary, a work of witness to the remarkable accomplishments in advanced visual culture—video and the new painting, sculpture and installation—that I had witnessed since my beginnings in writing some fifteen years before. The book was to be a mark on the ground, a pile of rocks telling other travellers on the desert route that I had come that far.

But almost immediately upon leaving *The Globe*—an event that coincided with leaving the bottle—and beginning to plan the book in the quietness of library and study, I began to experience the fearful, gradual drying and emptying I had known twenty years before. I struggled on with the project for a couple of months, watching artists' films, accumulating a vast archive of evidence about art in Toronto since the early 1970s, studying and reading. But throughout this time, there was a steady decline in my ability to *think* without inviting deluges of self-reproach and doubt.

Turning from research to writing, I found myself producing slabs of prose, dense and unreadable, void, without form or direction. I sought solace in research, groping among notecards with increasing desperation. It was like sweeping together feathers in a windstorm.

I tried an escape—this time, a trip to the South. It was disguised to myself and my wife as an occasion for visits with my dying sister, and for chats with an elderly, failing friend warehoused by her family in a cheap, desolate nursing home.

It was, in fact, a seeking for the dead Edwardian boy I had cut loose. On this summer trip, the constructed, confected mask of public, responsible creature I wore in Toronto could drop and die for a moment. I could go back to the graveyard of my Mays kin, carrying violets to my father's grave, a dead walk among the dead. I could wander alone through the deep woods in which I had sought refuge from the world as a child; in Greenwood again, I could be among the books and toys of my father, could feel the dry wooden propeller of his first airplane. I could sleep alone in his room, still lined with the amputated heads of the California deer and mountain sheep he had hunted and killed on his annual trips to America's western mountains fifty autumns before.

The slow decline into what would be the longest, darkest besiegement by the black dogs since the painful breakdown of 1969 began on the flight back to Toronto. It was then I saw a new truth, dead and bleak, the sort the dogs love: that there would be no book, no child of imagination, no product. Waiting for me in Toronto was only a void to be filled with unconvincing lies told to friends, dealers, colleagues, artists about a "book-in-progress" I knew was already dead, decaying inside me.

I could of course have announced the book's collapse freely when I returned to the newspaper in the summer of 1986. These things happen. No one, I imagine, would have thought much the worse of me for that. Had I been mentally well, such a course would have occurred to me. It did not. All I could think to do was avoid the subject of the book altogether. When interested acquaintances and co-workers insisted on asking, and refused to be put off by my diffidence, I began to back away from them, gradually cutting off contact. I saw people, even my bewildered friends, less and less, inventing reasons to dislike and reject and avoid them. I did not then know that such exaggerated sensitivities, such reluctance to let anyone touch or even know about the trivial wound, were drawing me back towards the ancient aloneness at the edge of the clearing.

———————

8 June 1986

sitting in a Southern Maid donut shop, writing, after an hour with Mrs. S in the nursing home, shrunk old woman helpless on iron bed

brought her a Whitman's Sampler—my grandmother told me 30 years ago it was Mrs. S's favourite kind of chocolate—

and I wonder if no book is to be made, nothing to be made that will not end here, on an iron bed, leaking away into non-existence

the bed is on wheels that turn and there is no end to their turning as they push the iron bed up the hall and down again

no book in me, not today anyhow—nothing to do but fail and fail and then there is the failing, falling into the iron bed on wheels that go around, and i cannot sleep here, any better than I could in Toronto—just wheels and no book and the not-making of going around in not sleeping

—i am so tired, more tired than the shrunk old woman, my friend, since she is dying and i am not, and there is so much tiring living to be done, going around and nowhere and anywhere—

———————

I spent much of the early spring of 1987 dreading an upcoming trip to Germany. It would involve a plunge into Documenta, one of the densest gatherings of successful art-world folk, hence into what I felt would be a nest of vipers. But if I had departed full of dread, I arrived in Kassel for that June's opening of Documenta spiritually intoxicated by a stopover in Rome, happier than I had been in years, free of the clinging torments of the summer before. I spent the first couple of days wandering among the myriad displays, discovering art again, luxuriating in it.

Then, gradually, came the usual brushes, encounters, chats with people known and unknown. At first, these engagements were pleasantly intriguing, a chance to eavesdrop on international gossip about art—to feel like a part of that world. Then the small grudges and petty hatreds that constitute so much of the art world's everyday interchange began to wear away at my naïve enthusiasm. That erosion continued until I suddenly became the direct, specific object of the gratuitous intellectual contempt so readily poured out on anyone who comes close enough to art, artists, dealers, and the platoons of collectors, curators, flunkies and hangers-on.

The occasion was a late-evening gathering of artists and collectors, critics and curators in a little Kassel restaurant. The idea of such huddles, I suppose, is for all parties to relax and unwind after hanging art or conducting interviews, writing reviews or making deals. For at least one bright, famously vicious artist, however, the dinner party was an opportunity to humiliate me publicly, in every way he could think of.

After some ten years as an art critic, I was certainly no stranger to such displays of hatred; and perhaps had I still been drinking and thereby partly insulated from this malice, I might have brushed aside the whole incident as merely another instance of art-world acting up. But I had no alcohol and what moral armour I possessed had been largely weakened and eaten away by my corrosive obsession with my failure to write the book. The event left me in a peculiar state—not of ordinary depression, but of something close to suicidal abjection, an overwhelming sense of utter worthlessness.

I left the restaurant, walked a friend back to his hotel, then returned to my own, and drank myself into vomiting stupor.

———————

12 June 1987

ugly box hotel room   drinking alone, nice—first time
to get drunk since i "quit drinking"—
*   german drunks falling down on the Straße street*
singing songs—raunchy i guess
*   me, getting drunk   first time in—can't remember*
how long
*   a few days ago Rome, so beautiful—then fly to*
Frankfurt, got a car   drove to Kassel   drove around
the witchy hills and black valleys
*   Grimm Bros. got their tales here in the witchy valleys*
and in the forests from the witches
*   Kassel   Documenta   is Kassel   and that's all it*
means to me
*   wanted to get here so i got here to see the art*
something beautiful for a change   maybe get it up
again for art
*   —tonight got clawed open by smart son of a bitch*
Canadian artist and that's the art world   get out of it
fucking artists, fucking art dealers and collectors
*   the whole fucking lot of them hating me and i can't*
help it
*   that's the art world and the clawing and now i know it*
*   them, hating me and I know I'm too stupid to*
understand anything about fucking art   got to get out
of here away from the people clawing at me

———————

In the months and years that followed my return from Europe in 1987, I was never to drink again. I did continue writing about art. But even as I had hidden myself away some twenty years before, I again began to abandon contact with the world beyond my doors to reduce the intensifying pain that seemed to begin with the episode in Kassel. It was an instance of the paradoxical, self-defeating way neurotics too often do things when faced with a decision, a slight or wound: increase the force of repression, resist the temptation to pleasure, thus only deepening and lengthening the terms of debilitating depression.

If the years that followed were marred by many lost hours and days, their desolation did not remotely approach that of the middle 1960s. This more recent season of turning inward was rich in discovery. My path lay then, and still lies, through the enchanted forest of German Romantic imagination, the terrain of Friedrich Hölderlin's poems, the paintings of Caspar David Friedrich, the operas of Richard Wagner and the art of Joseph Beuys and Anselm Kiefer in our own century. It was to find my path through this wood that I learned the German language, and continue to study it.

But even as these joys emerged in my life, the depressions came more often, dragging me down longer, into more desolate rings of the abyss. Nothing was left to protect me from the acute dread I have always experienced in *small* groups, or in situations of intimate interchange.

The especially heavy, prolonged depressions I suffered in the springs of 1990 and 1991 pushed me into wearying, worrying, sleepless anxiety, paralyzed me, and occasionally drove me near madness itself—the state I have always most feared, because I have believed that, once in that zone beyond life, there is no path back. I pushed friends away with insults and indifference, cold silences. Yet I did not pass over that threshold; I remained just this side of it, in that small terrain of real life on which I still had a purchase, however tentative, constricted, eccentric.

20 August 1991

the dogs came for me last night in my narrow bed.
  the other night they turned me into an animal.
  i am miserable tonight with fear that they will come
again for me, enter the room to bother me, lurk in
corners, keep me awake again with their nearness, the
silence of it.

the dogs came again for me last night, to suck the poison
from the tumour growing on my soul, as i die and pray,
dying towards the dark, and then unspeakable light.
  and now there are places for the dogs in my room,
must always be a place for them in my heart, a
welcoming hearth. they belong to me—i cannot forget
this—and they are not to be driven away with a stick,
lest they return and sit in the corner of the room,
frightening me into the sickness without end.

CHAPTER 7

Wisdom and Chemistry

early December, 1991

Near Christmas   feeling nothing for it, of it
 brittle tinkling like glass in my head
 tinkle brittle   snap, then silence
 Advent candles lit, burning bright on the wreath this
day—
 but were i to put my finger in, i could feel nothing—
 brittle finger made of metal
 zinc perhaps, a tapping sound on a window-pane and

*that would be me again, tip-toeing, tapping with a cold
gleaming zinc finger on the glass outside a house i do not
belong in—*

---

*I*t could have gone on forever, the secretive, withdrawn
life I lived after 1987, after the collapse of my book, in
that season of little hurts nursed into bleeding ulcers, never
leaving me free of pain for an instant. Unlike my driven and
confused spirit in the 1960s, my mind in this time was almost
too clear, too firmly fixed on certain goals. I continued both the
intensely private pursuit of specific forms of knowledge and my
highly public work as journalist and art critic—while between
these two ways of being in the world, there was opening an
increasingly barren field of dispassionate ground. Old intimacies
were disappearing, one by one.

There is, of course, a benign, wholly ordinary explanation for
at least some of this, one that does not rely on excuses grounded
in malignant melancholy and self-accusation. Margaret and I
were in our forties when our daughter Erin was born; and some
friends—particularly those whose children were grown up and
gone by that time, or who had young offspring of their own—
understandably had less time for us, and our novel, difficult,
delightful preoccupation with our young daughter. Unquestionably, we too had less time for our friends.

And as I have learned from the example of others, men
approaching fifty undergo a sometimes dramatic, but more
often subtle, change—a certain intensified concentration on
some final triumphant accomplishment, intellectual, sexual or
otherwise. It has to do, I assume, with the simple recognition
that most of life is gone, and that the time to do what we have
been putting off is now. In my case, these usual forces exacer-
bated my natural, probably harmless predilection for time alone
with my books or music. But such predictable behaviour was
being subtly compounded with darker movements of the spirit,

arising from my history of depression.

If, for example, I was vulnerable in my late forties to ordinary concerns about ambitions unfulfilled, I was also increasingly obsessed with my failures—to finish my doctorate in English, to complete the book on art begun in 1986, to attain true excellence as an art critic, to find a place of service in the Church, even to master German—a goal I should have known was impractical for anyone who had begun the study only a few years before. Little things, big things preoccupied me, stalling me in the peculiar churning that is depression's hallmark and calling card.

Had I seen clearly the creeping return of depression's full hegemony over me, I might have been able to face the fact that it was I, not a friend or acquaintance, who withdrew on the merest pretext, after the most harmless slight or discourtesy. Instead of dealing forthrightly with these incidents—and watching them melt like frost under the sun of honesty—I accumulated a pantry of grudges that provided excuses for not seeing this person, not attending that function, for pushing away new and old hands of friendship.

I have little doubt about what would have become of me had the pattern gone on unchecked. But an unrequested grace came to me on a chilly, busy afternoon in mid-December, 1991, changing everything.

---

15 December 1991

*woke up early this Sunday morning, had to make myself
do it—but drove out to Hilton Falls, and walked 20k
in the cold, all going by very quickly, feet moving as
though they did not belong to me—because all of it, so
beautiful—ragged sky tattered with grey clouds against
blue sky, clattering trees now naked of all leaves—
  but alone again:*

*and wondering into that aloneness as i wandered into
the rattling woods, wind-shivered, off the trail today,
losing myself for a while as i like to do, then always
finding something with my compass—*

*but wandering into aloneness is not that, with a
compass to save you—*

*Margaret says it has been four years now since i have
been unfrozen, a word off the page, bouncing in
language—4 years, that would be about right, 1987—
but i am so tired of everything now, of being a <u>current
word</u>*

*not preferable to being a dead one or an English one
that nobody says anymore:*

<u>*ybunden*</u>*...*

<u>*hrimcealde*</u>*...*

<u>*Hwæt!*</u>

The train of events that would eventually break the constricting
hold of my dark thoughts began with an urgent call from
Destinations, the now-defunct travel magazine of *The Globe and
Mail.* It was a rush request for a European story.

I had little doubt that I could come up with *something.* My
past work for *Destinations* had been happy and interesting,
though always carefully planned. I was intrigued by the notion
of sitting down and thinking up an effective story idea in one
go, flying off to Europe almost at once, coming back and writing
it up, all *tout de suite.* (Not incidentally, I had just turned fifty.)

My job was made easy by the sort of piece *Destinations*
wanted. It was to be about someplace in Europe set clanging by
the mighty bells then ringing in great political and social change
across the continent. My destination, I decided—and the editors
immediately agreed—would be Kiev. The focus of the story
would be the city's famous eleventh-century Sophia Cathedral,
which had been much in art-world news the previous autumn.

The grand lady in Kiev was caught in a powerfully symbolic crossfire between two forces vying for moral authority in the ruins of post-Communist Ukraine. On one side was a clutch of old-style state bureaucrats and museum professionals, determined to maintain their hold on this immensely historic "museum," with its precious mosaics and frescoes—the very embodiment, in microcosm, of the hated, haughty regime the Ukrainian people had overthrown, following the attempted Moscow coup the summer before. On the other side stood a multitude of ordinary worshippers, and, with them, the stolid, densely bearded and black-robed hierarchy of the Ukrainian Orthodox Church—former fellow-travellers perhaps, but now newly emboldened to stand up to secular authorities. Their ambition was to restore this focus of Ukrainian pride, secularized under Stalin and almost ripped down in the 1930s to discourage anti-Russian sentiments, to the status of a national house of prayer and solemn civil ceremony.

The dispute between the two camps had reached a climax in October, when Orthodox hunger-strikers camped out on the cathedral close and refused to be budged, and a platoon of museum officials holed themselves up inside the great church, also without food, determined that the Christians should not pass. A potentially violent collision of wills was averted by a fast huddle of top Orthodox clergy and state bureaucrats, who agreed to allow a single celebration of the Orthodox liturgy in the building, followed by a cooling-off period. The issue of the Sophia Cathedral's fate was still simmering when I left for Ukraine on the second day of January, 1992.

Kiev is the sort of ancient site of Christian worship— Glastonbury Abbey, Canterbury and Rome are others—I have always loved to visit. Its spiritual legacy stems from the tenth century, when the pagan warlord Vladimir decided to end the isolation of his rowdy warrior hoard from the imperium of

Orthodox Christendom by ostentatiously marching himself, his soldiery and the citizens of his fortress at Kiev into the Dnieper River for summary baptism into the Christian Church, and by implication, into the Christian Roman Empire.

Nowadays, it seems strange that the rough conversions typical in the European Dark Ages not merely took root, but flourished so gloriously. I know myself to be an heir of such conversions, first of my Romano-British forebears, then, a little later, of my Anglo-Saxon ones. The key to this durability, it appears, was what converts got as a result of their willy-nilly baptism: not merely exemptions from the displeasure of their newly Christianized warlord, but abrupt integration into a new, sophisticated culture.

And, sure enough, upon Vladimir's conversion of his principality of Rus, the land was flooded with the prestigious largesse of Byzantium: whole libraries, scholars and monks, priests to perform the breathtakingly beautiful rites of state and Church, lawyers and compendia of law, purveyors of imperial manners and mores, schools and monasteries and doctors. But even after this rapid influx of basic Christian civilization, there was still a gap to be filled. Coming to the throne in 1019, Prince Yaroslav, Vladimir's cultivated heir, found an official culture continuous with that of the Byzantium, but without any great buildings to show for it. So it was that the prince ordered architects from the imperial capital on the Bosphorus to construct an appropriately royal church on the pattern of the mighty cathedral of Holy Wisdom in Constantinople, fit for the anointing, crowning and burying of Christian Slavic princes. The result was the Sophia Cathedral.

By the time I arrived in Kiev, on the third day of Ukrainian independence, official atheism, and the requirement to be publicly atheistic in order to get up the career ladder, lay among other Leninist trappings in the ruins of the socialist regime. Even before the official New Year's Day break with Moscow, the once-secretly Orthodox faithful had been returning in droves to worship in the

few churches that had remained open throughout the Soviet
period, and were re-opening for prayer those that had been used
as state museums. Rag-tag companies of Orthodox monks,
young and old, in shabby black habits and with long, unkempt
hair, were coming back from heaven knows where, and simply
reoccupying the ancient monasteries shut down decades ago by
the Communists.

Of all the important shrines of Ukrainian Orthodox
Christianity, and of Ukrainian national pride—forces inextricably bound in ways Christians from the secularized West almost
instinctively find odd and somewhat menacing—the Sophia
Cathedral remained the most conspicuous point of conflict.

I expected to find the controversy interesting, and the beautiful frescos and mosaics of the Sophia enchanting; I did not
expect to be transfigured.

---

7 January 1993

*I write in my austere, socialist-realist tourist hotel after
a first day at Sophia Cathedral, being shown the place
by curators eager to impress. Words are hard to find for
the church—I am walking in Kiev, a certain foreign
city, familiar in its nineteenth-century architectural
comfortableness, however run down—but I am also
walking in a garden blazing yet unconsumed.*

*—everything is burning here, in this a garden on
fire—the mosaics and the very stones and plaster of the
churches, the icons, the mobbing crowds of worshippers
crowded into church for the Christmas liturgy, all
burning, smouldering with intense light and glory—
even the shabby monks in dirty black, young monks
with scanty beards, old holy men shuffling across
muddy lawns, are all burning, burning, smouldering
like coals—*

*—I feel that I am catching fire, I cannot touch
anything, touch a hand or wall without being burned
by the flickering fires of this place, its holiness—*

The Sophia Cathedral is a universe: its hemispheric profile echoes the bowl of sky, while the rounded brick, frescoed arches supporting its thirteen cupolas draw the rising eye gently back down to the floor, to the near and real. The visitor is not dwarfed but embraced, drawn from the unimpressive modern foyer into twilit aisles, defined by a forest of firm pillars, towards the central clearing, sunlit from the windowed dome high above.

In this clearing at the centre of the world is the Sophia's grandest survivor of Mongol looting, and four hundred subsequent years of neglect and ruination: the brilliant portrait, composed of innumerable gleaming glass tesserae, of the Mother of God, arms raised in prayer and victory.

Faced with this titanic figure, wrought in deep blue and burning gold glass, I found myself beholding a union as sublime as any I had ever seen: Pallas Athena, protectress of the city, countenance radiant with militancy, intelligence, love, merged with Mary, Mother, sheltering Earth and Sky. All the architectural sightlines and imposed decoration in the church led the eye back to this Virgin Warrior, the blazing incarnate Wisdom that has swept away all ignorance and superstition, conquered all foes in the name of joy, intelligence, freedom.

I do not know whether I would call what happened to me in the Sophia Cathedral a religious experience. Other people who have no religion at all report lightning flashes of insight and humility in the presence of the greatest Christian art. But of this I am certain: upon my first confrontation with Sophia's beauty, a sparkling tidal wave hurled itself against the tight, narrow fortress I had been building around my solitude, eroding its base in enmity. I recognized it, for I had experienced before the attack upon self-enforced littleness by the Beloved's magnanimity, the exquisitely intense beauty with which he has flooded the world, in the Church and through the Church's liturgy, learning and mercy. I had known before how quickly this stirring majesty can make easy, worldly compromise insipid, and the self-isolation of depression loathsome.

Alone on a high bluff above the Dnieper River one cold, sunny Kievan afternoon, I found myself thinking back to the crude miracle worked by Vladimir's baptism.

I imagined a man, myself a thousand years ago, secretly clutching his mute little idols and superstitions, being herded down the hill from the citadel with hundreds of other men and women, thence into the water. Next came his perfunctory plunge by bearded priests of the new religion, standing waist-deep in the muddy stream, saying words over his head in a language he did not understand as they pushed him under the shimmering surface.

Then came the raising of the man by strong arms from those depths, back into the sunshine. Perhaps he then just struggled back to shore, soggy, pagan still at heart, wondering what this obligatory performance had been all about. It would be years, if he lived so long, before he would witness the material and intellectual glories that were to come in the wake of the joining of his tribal band to imperial Christian *Romanitas*. And, even should he live to see such wonders, he might never know the Beloved's loveliness.

But if this imaginary Slavic warrior had been differently inclined, he might have emerged from the Dnieper waters changed, aware of the new life dawning upon his people and land. Perhaps he was bewildered by the procedures of this elaborate new religion, not wholly comprehending the change that had been wrought in him, but filled with a spiritual hunger. Perhaps the new convert went back to family and friends to work out his salvation there, and await the imperial glories of culture, art, architecture yet to come—to wait for the revelation of that greater Glory he had glimpsed in the sparkle of sunshine on the waters of baptism into larger life.

Cramped by years of distancing myself, shrunken morally and emotionally by self-imposed isolation and pride, I suddenly wanted to be the second of my two imaginary converts, the one who saw the Beloved's reflection in the waters of baptism, and never ceased searching for the Original. But if I could not be him, I would be a man of the other sort, continuing in ignorance, groping, longing.

In my depressed state, I realized, I could be neither man. In any case, I knew from that moment I had to begin the slow conversion, the gradual baptism of my soul and awakening to love all over again, in the waters of my own homeland.

———

January, 1992
Christmas   Kiev:

> the living dogma, the blazing bread, <u>moral</u> beauty—
> I have seen it face to face, and lived—
>   i have seen the hints, must have seen them, the traces
> or fragments, in bits of broken mirror all my life or i
> would not have recognized it there—the beauty of the
> Beloved itself, scattered in fragments perhaps for our
> sakes: for we could not live with our eyes fixed steadily
> on that furnace—
>   yet i have seen it, in the fleshly, hairy quiddity of what
> i am, sexual and basic, and have lived to write this—for
> God so loved the world that he clothed his son in its hair
> and flesh—to listen to that, to see it, as I have, in Kiev,
> is to be embodied, created, exactly as I am, the sexual,
> emotional <u>whatness of it</u>.

> *the vision forbids loathing of desire, the body the thing*
> *it is. no danger: "for we know that nothing can separate*
> *us from the love that is in Christ Jesus."*
>   *the vision forbids the hatred of the brittle bit sitting*
> *here writing this of It, of Her   the vision opens and*
> *opens and opens again, Mary opening towards me,*
> *allowing, endlessly allowing—*

By the end of my visit to Kiev, I was furious. As far back as I could remember, depression had been ruining every human delight for me, including the profligate delights offered by great art and music, even nature itself.

Many of these pleasures, I had simply learned to live without. I could not be a gardener, because I could not feel the beauty of flowers; I could never enjoy the night sky. Even treks through the forests around Berlin—perhaps the closest I had ever come to simply enjoying myself—were often wrecked by the incessant rattling of resentments, the recollection of long-past hurts and slights, the webs of malice and conspiracy I spun around myself. But the great icon in the Sophia Cathedral had reminded me of a beauty that no hatred, on earth or in hell, can defeat, alloy, dilute. There, by the Dnieper, I vowed to fight the black dogs, by whatever means I could find and to the death if need be.

By the time I returned to Toronto, my anger had inclined towards histrionics. I was, or believed myself to be, prepared to do anything—fast within an inch of starvation, go on toilsome pilgrimages, begin some martial routine of prayer and meditation—*anything* rather than lose the memory and the experience of that beauty glimpsed in Kiev.

I decided to return to Dr. Rosen, after several seasons of absence, and do what I had never before done: give him an ultimatum. If a treatment for my deep, enduring anhedonia existed, I told him—treatment however radical or frightening or unproved—I was ready to try it: hydrotherapy, a punishing diet of sprouts and grains, electroconvulsive shock therapy, the lock-up in a psychiatric hospital, dosages of drastic, mind-bending drugs. I knew that the disease robbing me of the ability to feel joy may well be incurable or untreatable. And yet I resolved to fight it all the same, outside the psychiatric transaction altogether if need be. If you can't do anything, I told Dr. Rosen furiously, then I am out, never to return, and never to stop knocking on the doors of medical doctors, mind doctors, spiritual healers, acupuncturists and pyramidologists until I find someone who will give me the equipment to keep the desolation at bay a little longer, a little better.

After this melodramatic performance, received by my psychiatrist with his usual taciturn, half-bemused composure, he said he would begin seeing me again weekly, scribbled out a prescription, and gave it to me with the words: Try this.

Had I been a responsible depressive, keeping up with current research on the disorder's causes and treatment, or even a reader of newsmagazines or the medical stories in my own newspaper, or if I watched television even occasionally, I would have recognized that the green-and-cream capsules the pharmacist handed me contained Prozac. Before reading it on the bottle in the pharmacy that morning in early 1992, I don't recall ever having seen the word.

---

2 February 1992

—*on contemplation of the good (natural virtue):*
"*think on these things,*" *suggests St. Paul (in*
<u>Phillipians</u>, *Ch.4, verse 8)—*

alēthē	*the actual, true, unconcealed*
semna	*the venerable, serious, grave*
dikaia	*the right*
agna	*the holy, pure, the uncontaminated*
prosfilē	*the pleasing, agreeable lovely*

eufēma the fair-sounding
arete kai epainos the virtuous, what is commended.

perhaps now i shall be able to think on these things,
all my desire now, all towards which my heart tends
in its wandering way across the green hills

On a bitterly cold, snowy February morning in 1992 I downed my first forty milligrams of Prozac. For the few days following, I felt nothing, good or ill. The mildly malicious side-effects Dr. Rosen had warned me to watch out for—headaches, dry mouth and so forth, all of which usually accompany the first week or so on any antidepressant medication—did not come. Nor did any abrupt upswing of mood.

Then, after a little more than a week, I began to chirp. Which is not the same thing as becoming gradually more cheerful. I simply woke up one morning at 5 a.m., my usual hour, pulled on the tattered work-clothes I wear when writing at home, stumbled upstairs to the kitchen and began the routines of the day— putting together the morning's first cappuccino, warming a blueberry muffin in the microwave—when I suddenly became aware of the rain. It was cold, wind-whipped winter rain, dancing hard on the large glass skylights over the upper floor of our loft—a sound to which I had, to that moment, been either indifferent or mildly hostile. This time, however, it struck me as a sound more beautiful than any natural one I had ever heard. The north wind smiting and rattling the windows, the chilly droplets of rain beating down through the pre-dawn dark on the glass skylight above the kitchen, were a sonic experience symphonic in the most literal sense, every voice and timbre of the rainstorm perfectly matching every other.

Deciding it was altogether too lovely a sound to keep secret, I ran down the stairs, woke my wife, and told her to get dressed and come listen to the rain. Margaret, no morning person, heaved over, pulled the duvet up around her chin, and went back to sleep. I was left to listen to the music of the rain alone, which I did for hours, lying on the sofa under the skylights until the dawn crept under the low, heavy clouds, and the showers gradually tapered off and ceased.

––––––––––––

This euphoria, common at the outset of any course of therapy with antidepressant medicines, was probably not good for me, and certainly was not good for my wife, who threatened to flush my entire stash down the toilet if I did not stop twittering about every minor pleasure that came my way.

Fortunately for my marriage, the frothy elation lasted less than a couple of weeks, then gradually subsided. By the end of about a month, the drug had begun to work more or less as the medical literature suggested it would for some chronically depressed people, at least some of the time: it slowed the swings of the emotional pendulum, instilled the ability to take pleasure in ordinary things, and, most important, laid a firm bottom on the dreaded, previously bottomless well of despair into which depressives fall at the worst moments. Prozac had given me the pleasure of early-morning rain on the skylights. It had also given me enough peaceable spirit to resume my old practice of saying, and finding deep joy in, the Church's readings, prayers and thanksgivings, at dawn and at dusk—the simple, lovely Christian acts, the recapturing of which had led me to seek chemical help in the first place.

And Prozac, for a time, rinsed me clean of the scent of prey: the black dogs prowled elsewhere throughout the spring and early summer of 1992, when I expected them to make their worst annual predatory excursion into my territory. For months I woke up each morning able to see sunlight falling through a frosty window on scarlet hibiscus blossoms, ready to hear, to sense, all kinds of beauties occluded before with thudding regularity.

The maddening hamster-cage of resentments, grudges and poisonous anxieties that whir inside the brains of depressed people, the bilious dwelling upon tiny slights and hurts that had absorbed hours and days of my life during the previous four years, all slowed, then largely stopped. In their stead were pleasurable things that had been little more than a rumour up to that point: the crisp rustle of a duvet being readied for kindly sleep, the plunge of hoe and shovel into the chilly ground in spring.

---

30 May 1992

*Late to be starting a garden on the deck, late to be
writing about it in this, my first garden diary, late in
life, and in the course of things—but today was right
and lovely: The heavy wooden boxes finished, the dirt
put in, and, under heavy rain, the first day of planting.*
    Ideas vanishing before the fact,
      *plans left behind as the facts conspire to make them
irrelevant*
    *as the dirt and water and feeble, ugly little green
things went in, the scraps the garden books make seem so
lovely, and perhaps they shall be, before summer's end.
A very homely thing indeed, buxom crates graceless with
sodden expanses of pseudo-dirt, punctuated by limp
sprigs. It is odd, how impossible it is to believe that
any of this will turn into something beautiful.*
    *But today the first visitor sat in the fresh-planted white
birch tree: a sparrow, proletarian of birds, but a bird
nonetheless; hence very welcome in this secret place
above the city rooftops.*

My earliest experiences with Prozac, strange and wonderful and new, inspired none of the particular brand of curiosity (fussy, pedantic, microscopic, technical) that I usually bring to hobby or personal enterprise.

I knew nothing first-hand of psychopharmacology, since I had never, before Prozac, taken mind-medicine of any sort. (It had always been Dr. Rosen's position that the side-effects of most standard antidepressants available before Prozac were worse than depression itself.) For that matter, I had never taken the slightest interest in any prescription drugs, including the ones I had taken for years to prevent high blood pressure from blowing off the top of my head. But, then, there is nothing tangible, experientially *real*, about chronic high blood pressure, nothing to inspire interest in the mind of its victim. Consciousness does not register symptoms of even severe hypertension (until the disease abruptly kills or cripples you), nor does it note any effects when the vessels relax and pressure comes down.

In contrast, the onset of even a mild spell of depression is immediately dreadful. And whether mild and gradual or drastically swift, the experiential content is the same: a drift or rush towards the erasure of joy, the erosion of the will to live or even to desire, to love or respond to love. And whether the coming of relief is dramatic, or not, the exact timing, and the button that sets it in motion, are always mysterious.

As I was to discover, the oddity of depression is imbued with a kind of suspicious magic when the withdrawal of black dogs begins almost immediately—and quite unbelievably—after starting to knock back two tiny, expensive capsules each morning. Though they had been prescribed to have precisely that effect, I would not have believed it possible before experiencing it myself. I was, for the first time in my career as an uncurious depressive, curious about my disorderly inner life and the peculiar straightenings, quietings now at work within it.

---

18 August 1992

*High summer, late in fact at this latitude—but all that
the green things were supposed to have done, they did,*

*and I sit now among them, in their loveliness of white
and blue and violet blossoms, the many greens of tree,
shrub, creeping plants, resplendent vines, thinking of
<u>genius loci</u>.*

*The deck: planking over a roof, and beneath that my
study full of books, and beneath that our bedroom, on
broadloom, over concrete, and concrete over the ancient
clay bed of Lake Iroquois, drained when the surface of
that vast glacial puddle sank, becoming Lake Ontario.*

*A flat deck-top, roof-line, opening towards the south
over the old lakebed that cannot be seen, since the city
came and buried the streams and rivers, slashed down
the forests, drove away north the bear and deer.*

*For a little while, a field; then, in 1912 or so, came
the little houses of my street, covering the flatland
abruptly, except for one vacant lot, where a tool-and-die
shop would be built, and in which I live today. A
factory, used to make things until things were made
no more in Toronto, and the derelict building was
reoccupied by makers of information—words, visual
images, architectural forms, this diary, the evanescent
stuff of culture*

—reoccupied by us.

<u>*Genius loci*</u>*: a deck that is also a roof, secret tree-house,
roofless belvedere open to stars and sky; a recollection of
the clearings that opened within the forests here not two
centuries ago. Above: the most rapidly changing weathers
in the world, ever being transformed by the world-
encircling river of wind, the jet stream. Below: my
parapet and garden aloft. Within: Cain the fallen man,
the gardener not by choice, <u>made</u> to civilize. Abraham
Cowley: "God the first garden made, and the first city,
Cain..."*

*But my garden, a contradiction of sorts to the city.
A building of a negative altar, a space in the grove of*

> *culture that is* <u>*itself*</u> *a kind of culture, yet with one*
> *difference: that it is not a closing towards the lights and*
> *temperatures and weights of humidity, as the modern*
> *building is. It is the city that is tame; the garden must*
> *be wild, oblique, a cut across the utopia of urbanism,*
> *this Babel we build because we fear...*

An aversion to dwelling on my disorder had kept me from stocking up on books about it, despite the fact that they seemed to fill shelf after shelf in the "psychology" sections of bookshops everywhere. But an even more powerful disincentive was the content of the books themselves. After reading a few self-help books, enough to form a general opinion, I categorized them as, by and large, the mischievous work of three sorts of people.

The first, and perhaps most numerous, are mere charlatans and pirates, deliberately soaking depression's unhappy victims of the only power we are occasionally left with, the power of money.

The second kind of self-help purveyors are for the most part, I believe, at least partly well-meaning, dreamily pious or merely bouncy pepper-uppers, whom someone has flattered into believing that their "insights" or "techniques" are novel, wondrous, potentially helpful to multitudes of sufferers. Ignorant of the depths of depression's roots in self, psyche and language, oblivious to depression's supple resistance to happy talk, committed to sparing the depressed the often frightening medical treatments prescribed for this disorder, these writers cannot be helpful; but neither are they, by and large, particularly harmful.

And their nostrums do, perhaps, perk up some mildly, temporarily blue readers, and get them back on track. The only persons whom such books may harm are the desperately depressed still unaware of the stubbornness of their disorder. The harm is in the giving of false hope—usually from a position on high; for what depressive would read a book by a help-dispenser who admitted being miserable, destitute, in punishing loneliness, and empty of affection? The harm done to readers will never be known—since those for whom the gods fail, the nostrums evaporate, the flimsy rope up to the light at the top of the well of darkness suddenly breaks, are not the people public-relations departments seek out to give testimonials to the miracle cure.

The third and by far the most dangerous creators of self-help books are the certified mind doctors, the professionally trained psychiatrists and psychologists who've turned writers, or—a not uncommon practice, I understand—hired ghosts to write their books for them. Their academic credentials, often impeccable and impressive, and their sophisticated-sounding writing give their texts stature in the minds of intelligent depressives who would otherwise be disinclined to pay attention.

Particularly, the doctors' numerous references to clinical practice lend the weight of authority, the ring of inevitable truth, to what they proclaim. At the heart of this proclamation is the claim that what they are writing is certainly not cheap self-help, not trendy feel-good uplift, but a truth that can drive away the clouds of terror.

———

5 September 1992

most perfect of late summer days—skies clear and
fathomless blue, sunshine warm on my face but leaving
the air cool, still—the first day in weeks i walked in
the woods, off on the side-routes—
*   —the opening of the path through the woods, trees*
arching overhead, abundances of yellow, blue and golden
wildflowers, apples coming to blush on wild trees at the
edge of farmers' fields, all of it more missed than i could
have imagined—

———

My hunt for the story of Prozac began with a dive into the serious literature most accessible to lay people: the standard clinical compendiums on library reference shelves, medical histories of melancholia and depression and related disorders, and their cultural representations.

My first reaction to the necessary reading was wonderment, not at any matter strictly chemical or psychiatric, but at the riches English gives to scientific officialdom for expressing its uncertainty, doubt, reservation, its lack of commitment to "fact" while it ponderously asserts privileged truth.

No newspaper reporter would be allowed to get away with such tactics. One wonders how the writers of technical medical manuals would survive even routine editorial scrutiny of the expressions indispensable to their craft—the slippery little modifiers such as "perhaps" and "supposedly," or those vague and disabling grammatical structures, usually formed by casting active verbs into their subjunctive moods—tricks that allow them to assert grave matters authoritatively, while leaving open the possibility that their claims may be worthless.

For while Prozac does something experimentally verifiable to the body, it is not clear why or how this makes any difference in the mood of the body taking it. And the professional literature on Prozac (or fluoxetine hydrochloride, to give the drug its chemical honours) and serotonin (the target-substance in the neural network on which fluoxetine homes in) is a murky swamp of "maybe" language.

The hesitations are not new. While an atmosphere of cautious approval has pervaded the discussion of the newest generation of antidepressants, the papers prepared for an international symposium on the matter at London's Royal Society of Medicine in 1981—to cite merely one of many such gatherings convened during the decade running up to Prozac's 1987 launch on the market—do not conceal a certain buzz of puzzlement. The attending researchers admitted trouble in establishing "a causative relationship between the defective serotonin transport system mechanism and depression." Understandably, they were wringing their hands over the conflict between the existentially upbeat tales told by depressives undergoing fluoxetine experiments and the "contradictory, inconclusive and difficult to interpret" laboratory data.

Some fifteen years later, and eight years after Prozac's meteoric rise to celebrity, the mystery of fluoxetine's actions and final effects has not yet been solved. The 1992 edition of *The Pharmacological Basis of Therapeutics*, one of those indispensable textbooks medical students have at their elbows, states flatly that "the neurotransmitter hypothesis of mood disorder" remains just that, an hypothesis; "the data are inconclusive and have not been consistently useful either diagnostically or therapeutically."

Yet more doubt was to be cast on the causality by the fourth and most up-to-date edition of the American Psychiatric Association's *Diagnostic and Statistical Manual of Mental Disorders* (1994)—the famous *DSM-IV*—which allows how a number of neurotransmitters are probably "implicated in the pathopsychology" of depression, serotonin among them. The writers hedge their bets, however, by adding that "no laboratory findings" support a direct connection between Prozac and relief from major depression. The pharmaceuticals giant Eli Lilly, in its tiny-type technical brochure intended for dispensing physicians, will go no farther out on the limb than to say that "the antidepressant action of fluoxetine is presumed to be linked to its inhibition of CNS [central nervous system] neuronal uptake of serotonin."

———

23 October 1992

    a soft, sunny afternoon, golden with autumnal radiance
      perfect for doing what i have to do: rip out the last,
    faded annuals of my first summer's garden, whack back
    the perennials, tump out and clean the water garden,
    bring the goldfish inside—

> *it does seem that a great many flowers i put in have*
> *disappeared along the way, but there is so very much*
> *for me to learn about all this—*
>   *about this, and the flourishing inside my head, the*
> *chemistry i may or may not continue to study this*
> *winter—there are more interesting things to do: ready*
> *the tools, calculate the amount of mulch to buy come*
> *spring, plan and draw off designs for what i shall try*
> *in the tiny terrain created on the deck—*
>   *a sad day, in all its tender beauty and cool, resolved*
> *beatitude—for this has been something i have always*
> *wanted to do, this gardening—and only now "gotten*
> *around to it," as the liar in me used to say—never had*
> *time for it, because of the endless depression, would be*
> *the truthful way to say it—*
>   *nightfall, rapidly falling as it becomes dark so early:*
> *brilliant electrical storms crackling to the west, heavy*
> *downpours on the way, showering down wind-blown*
> *into calm autumnal sleep—*

Leaving the murky jungle of maybe-language and re-emerging into the clearing of certainty, I found at least this much is true: ingested fluoxetine demonstrably affects the bodily chemical called *serotonin*, the shorthand handle given the chemical compound *5-hydroxytryptamine*. This substance, emitted from neural cell endings into the synapses between cells, is found throughout the human body in concentrations that vary from scant to considerable, depending on the neighbourhood. (It is found in anything with a neural system, including leeches, which receive from it their voracious appetite for blood.)

The existence of serotonin had been detected in blood samples more than a decade before 1948. But in that year, Cleveland researchers defined its chemical structure and gave the chemical its handy name by cobbling together the words *serum*, the ingredient of blood in which it was first located, and *tone*, the tautness and resilience serotonin induces in blood vessels and the musculature in the lining of other hollow organs, such as the lungs and intestines. (Certain rare tumours are known to produce serotonin and dump it into the bloodstream at a remarkable clip, intensifying muscular constrictions in these organs, thereby giving sufferers such symptoms as wheezing.)

Shortly after its isolation from blood serum and its descriptive chemical analysis, serotonin was discovered at work in neural synapses within the brain. This was not a big surprise. But it offered empirical confirmation of an elegant model of neural operations elaborated in the 1930s by Sir Henry Dale, an Englishman, and an Austrian scientist named Otto Loewi.

The Dale-Loewi model struck me as interestingly old-fashioned. Since ancient times until the middle of the last century, students of the body believed that information was conveyed throughout the body by "subtle fluids." Even Luigi Galvani, who announced in the 1790s the existence of "animal electricity" after his famous experiments with frogs, thought he was talking about a new sort of fluid.

It was not until the midst of the Victorian period, when electricity was being understood with increasing clarity that the physiologists overthrew the ancient learning. The work of nerves was done, the Victorians proclaimed, not by "subtle fluids" but by "nerve force" analogous, if not identical, to electricity. "It became common-place," an historian of neural science has written, "to compare the gray matter of the brain, generating nerve force, to a voltaic battery producing electricity, with the nerve fibers taking the part of electric wires, conducting power throughout the body." As recently as the Edwardian period, doctors believed that applying electricity to the bodies of depressed patients would restore the "nerve energy" apparently missing.

Not so, said the Englishman and the Austrian. The crucial transaction in the intricate messaging system causing my fingers to type these words, your hands to hold this book, your eyes to move along the line of type, is not electrical in nature at all, but chemical—fluid, in fact. Now electricity is indeed implicated in the exceedingly precise behaviours and manoeuvres our bodies perform, but only *within* the neuron. Upon reaching the end of a given nerve-cell, the interior flash of electricity induces myriad tiny packages of chemicals, called neurotransmitters, to rush to the cell-ending, where they then fire molecules of chemical into the tiny gap between nerve and nerve.

Put in vulgarly simple language—so simple that the marvellously intricate human brain has every right to be insulted as I write these words—the message is conveyed when these molecules brush against receptors in the receiving end of the next nerve down the neural line. Having done their job, some of these molecules are destroyed by enzymes floating in the synapse, while the rest are sucked back into the emitting cell, and wiped out by enzymes there—all this, to keep neurotransmission under exact control. Thus, the signals creating the muscle contractions which, in turn, create the letters on my computer screen are inhibited from making me now type the word *screen* ten thousand times, or until I drop dead of exhaustion.

For uncovering this exquisitely tuned, elegant system, Dale and Loewi were jointly awarded the Nobel Prize in 1936, nearly twenty years before the message-runners began to be isolated, structurally understood and given discrete names, one by one. Scientists concerned with the brain and body chemistry are now agreed that, whatever else it is and does, serotonin is one of several neurotransmitters running the innumerable errands that must be completed each second for the body and mind to run right.

---

16 December 1992

> *soft snow outside now at dawn, not quite so much as an
> hour ago, when i awoke in the darkness
> Advent, in the Church's ancient parsing of the year—*

time of first snows, the dreaded busywork of weeks before
Christmas, the abrupt quiet after the Nativity, and
peace in reading the daily prayers and psalms, the
ancient hymns, of Christmastide—
   on the deck, in the garden: the last debris of summer's
chrysanthemum rumpled under snow, dead tangles of
clematis sagging sadly under the weight of it, and i have
untended it all, leaving everything for later, whenever
that comes, if it ever does—
   winter's garden, in its way, is no less beautiful
than summer's—all is alive there, withdrawn into
hiddenness, being with God in his absence under
snow's cold coverlet—
   and it was a year ago, about now, that the plan to go
to Kiev came up, and i went, into that mystery still not
understood quite clearly, in its wondrous gilt and
glory—royal joys of a year ago, enjoyed in part for
themselves, in part because of the distances they drew
between me and technological modernity, the rootlessness
i know, God knows in his un-becoming, the sleeping
clematis roots on the deck does not know, being <u>in</u>
<u>*ground*</u>*—*

The good news for the pharmaceuticals industry came in the
early 1960s, when brain researchers noted that people afflicted
by depression and obsessive-compulsive disorders also happen to
have less serotonin in the right places—the synapses, that is—
than people who report no such symptoms. A flurry of laboratory busy-work was set in motion by this fingering of what
looked like a link between serotonin deficiency in the brain and
the odd drizzle of tears, the thoughts of dying and death, the
decline of ability to enjoy things experienced by untold millions.

Billions of dollars were spent on the quest for the psychoactive Pill To End All Pills. The race was won in 1972 by Eli Lilly

of Indianapolis with the invention of a substance researchers dubbed fluoxetine, presumably so they would not have to say *(±)-N-methyl-3-phenyl-3-[(∂,∂,∂-trifluro-p-tolyl)-oxy]-propylamine hydrochloride* every time the topic came up in the lunch room. Fluoxetine's claim to a famous place in the history of mind treatment rests on its undoubted power to increase the amount of serotonin at the junctures between neurons, while leaving other neurotransmitters to get on with their jobs unaffected. This it does by inhibiting the neuron's tendency to suck back up and destroy the emitted serotonin. When this inhibition is effective, people feel better. Nobody knows why.

By the mid-1980s, fluoxetine had successfully passed the usual battery of exhaustive tests on animals and humans required by United States government agencies and the scientific establishment, and surpassed expectations in several ways. It inhibited serotonin re-uptake as predicted, and also made at least sixty-five to seventy per cent of the chronically depressed people who took it in clinical trials say, and behave as though, they felt better about themselves and their world—more focused, less scatter-brained and distracted, and less subject to the dominion of obsessive-compulsive routines. Moreover, its use seemed to diminish the calamitous slides into the dark pits of depression that serotonin-short people, including this one, fear terribly.

But would so wondrous a drug eventually poison us, as so many of its predecessors had been found to do? Toxicity is the dark shadow-brother of effectiveness, and is a concern with any new drug, especially one that seems otherwise very promising. Fluoxetine, however, has so far behaved with streamlined courtesy towards all other substances and systems it was not sent in to deal with, demonstrating smart-bomb accuracy on the inhibition of serotonin re-uptake. And since suicide is rarely far from the mind of a depressed person, the clinicians were particularly pleased to find that fluoxetine is very reluctant to kill someone who has decided to swallow a handful of it.

The pre-release trials also suggested few fluoxetine users would be afflicted by the usual, variously unpleasant or destructive side-effects associated with previous popular anti-depressants, ranging from extreme fatigue and dizziness and heart trouble to dry mouth and constipation. Because Lilly's product had shown itself to be a safe, easy to take, reliable, non-addictive, admirably effective improver of the biographies of depressed people, it was accorded the *nihil obstat* of the U.S. Food and Drug Administration. In 1987, under the trade-name Prozac, the chemical was given its first nudge towards fame, controversy, and almost apocalyptic expectations among doctors and patients—none of which I knew about when I first began to take it.

Prozac struck me as wonderful in those first months, because of the almost immediate lifting of symptoms that had ruined countless hours of my life. It gave me hours that would have otherwise been lost. It gave me a garden. I expected it to go on giving me peace and inner bounty. It did not.

CHAPTER *8*

Giving In

29 March 1993

*...desire flickers, then burns itself into nothing, black
smudge on the damp ground...the idealism of what I
should be, turning on me with clean fangs to tear and
destroy...*

 a weightless, odd time of not knowing where i am—

 *on the deck, the ancient rhythms repeat, leaf-buds of
clematis swelling, a tiny flourish of sage-green thrift
leaves above the icy mulch—*

181

*i cannot do what I had hoped, any of it—this is the
end again, what i never hoped would come again,
   of hard waking and troubled sleep,
   and looking at the first swelling and greening of the
garden after the winter without feeling anything for it,
about it—not wishing to tend or even see this surge from
the inner heart of the world i am apart from—and on
the edges of the clearing, here, memories of matters past
creep back, invisible yet casting their dark shadows—the
bitterness, returned, and i understand so little*

---

*T**he** black dogs returned on a morning in March,
1993, as I gazed at witch-fingers of ice descending
from the deck above my study. Droplets of water dripped slowly
from their ends. A year before, that sign of spring's coming had
given me swift, unfamiliar pleasure, much quickening of spirit
and expectation. This time around came no sense of beginning,
merely the descent of a dread I had almost forgotten.

And with the dogs came the old complaints—the lassitude,
the dragging feet, the lowering fog of hopelessness, then the terrible words, bright, sharp, cruel. They were strangest of all. I had
not heard the language of self-hatred in my head, at least not this
clearly or authoritatively, for many months. Before the repertoire
of hateful terms and images was again laid at my feet that March,
they had come to seem very remote, barely recollected blots in
the diaries from days before Dr. Rosen first prescribed the mysterious capsules that would make everything so different, for so
long.

I was still nearly mute from the sheer oddity of this turn
when I received an unusual invitation. It came from my friend
and colleague Anne Collins, senior editor of *Saturday Night*, a
century-old magazine devoted to informing the educated
Canadian public on matters of general interest. Anne had known
about my depressions and knew of my recent experiences with

Prozac, but curiously, she did not call me directly. Instead, the call went to Margaret, a discreet query whether she thought I would consider writing about so intimate a topic as ruinous psychological disorder.

The notion that depression is often felt to be shameful was, of course, not off the mark. Nor was Anne's belief that I might not be willing to unveil myself as fully as would be required by such writing. Simply because it feels like moral failure, a lack of basic virtue—even if they know better—many depressives just don't want to talk about it.

What my friend at *Saturday Night* did not know—because it had never occurred to me to tell anyone—was that my first round of psychotherapy, years before, had released me from the particularly malignant illusion that depressives are personally culpable for their disorder. I knew I had done nothing to deserve chronic depression, nor was there anything that could spare me from it. The discovery that depression is incurable, its causes unknown, the outcome of its treatment uncertain at best, had freed me of all guilt.

It was an interesting invitation. I was being asked to *write depression*—not whine about its ruining of my life, not stand aloof and talk "objective" science I only half-understood, not come up with learned analysis of the controversies then stirring around fluoxetine therapy. My job was to compose a narrative that would be an analogue of the disorder itself—faithful to the "facts" of my situation as I unfaithfully, only half-realistically recalled them. It would be true in the way neurotic narrative is true, which is never more than partly.

Prozac had failed me, or at least its good effects had been overwhelmed by other tensions snatching at the complicated fabric of depression. Despite this, drumming up energy to write the article was not difficult, because it was a challenge of the sort any writer likes: to do something never attempted by him. In my case, I wanted to find out if I could write about a pervasive personal problem with neither self-pity nor self-aggrandizement.

So I took the job—but not because I believed my article would help end depression's predatory thefts of joy from my life or from anyone else's, and not because I believed I would put a dent in the business of the self-helpers, miracle curists and other charlatans. I took it because I thought that *writing* depression might bring me a step closer to learning to *rewrite it*—to construct new scripts so that the old, shabby ones could be discarded, or at least edited to make them easier to perform without a stammer.

----

19 April 1993

Writing now after a trip to nursery to get a lilac, and a white clematis ordained to bloom in autumn, silver lace—yet can hardly think, hold a thought in my head, because of the misery there, stirring.

Woke up this morning crying—unable to think a word, a sentence, ahead—Will have to quit work at the paper for the week, and how I hate myself for that— failing on all fronts, spiritual, intellectual, literary—

and this reading, for the article—where is it taking me? what does it mean? what sorcery is it working on my disarrayed mind? I would become another man, leave the old one behind, a moving fiction with a history devoid of the downturns, regrets losses frustrations rages—and time draining away into the insatiable ground—

But there remains in this room, writing these words, a man who remembers the room is wonderful, lined with uncounted volumes of ideas, musical sounds, images—who could put down roots deep in this soil and draw mind's nourishment from the images and books, like a plant from sun water soil and air—if there were not the draining away, the seepage of thought into the

*ground, and into this reading that is murkier, even
murkier—*

As I have already mentioned—the point is worth making again, since I would dissuade anyone from following my example—I am a bad psychiatric patient. I have never made it my business to keep up with research and theoretical work in the several overlapping fields of inquiry that touch upon depression. Anyone suffering from this disorder *should* have known, by 1992, about fluoxetine. And anyone writing about depression in the spring of 1993 *should* have been at least aware of the outpouring of books and articles about, and the widespread quickening of public interest in, this common malady.

I began my own article with some knowledge of the technical literature on psychoactive drugs, including Prozac, but in near-ignorance of the popular fascination with both the drugs and the disease. Only after the piece had been published in the November 1993 issue of *Saturday Night*, precipitating an avalanche of mail and a deluge of phone calls that bewilders me still, did it occur to me that my experience was one of interest to numerous people, depressed and undepressed alike. As I was to discover after the article came out, there is no shortage of published scripts for how to ride out depression, but very little writing from the inside—a place where there are no solutions and no promises of deliverance. While I certainly did not try to do so, I had created a literary curiosity, a text on chronic depression without answers, but also without questions; a narrative about everyday life on the planet of depression.

And yet, if writing the article convinced me that no cure *can* exist for a disorder that circulates through the social web of language and power, it also confirmed certain intuitions, and justified a few fears.

One has to do with every depressive's compulsive desire for assurance that he or she is indeed a failure. In the day-to-day life of a depressive, there can never be too much demoralization. Nor is there ever any shortage of it. During the modern era, a new army of tormentors has come of age, professional pessimists pouring discouragement into the centrifuge of mass culture and providing ample reinforcement for despair.

There is not a chronic depressive on earth, I suspect, who has not been instructed by somebody that he or she is just a complainer, an unsick whiner who simply does not wish to face up to life's ordinary discontents and losses. But if printed confirmation is wanted, publishers have numerous products for us self-absorbed "improvement" addicts, sunk in what the American historian Christopher Lasch has called a "culture of narcissism."

In the famous 1979 jeremiad that bears this title—a book that gives clear expression to received opinions, and propagates no new ideas—Lasch discovers narcissistic decadence and the breakdown of social courage everywhere. Even, alas, in Canada, "long a bastion of stolid bourgeois dependability." Back home in the U.S.A., he finds political liberalism intellectually and morally bankrupt, no longer able "to explain events in the world of the welfare state and the multinational corporation." Academia is in ruins; "philosophers no longer explain the nature of things or pretend to tell us how to live." Yea, even "economic man" himself—the great, noble creative fiction of the secularizing nineteenth century—has been displaced by something Lasch calls, with contempt, "psychological man."

This is the new narcissist of Lasch's title, a person "haunted not by guilt but by anxiety"—not by the frustration of noble aims, that is, but by free-floating, self-centred *angst.* This repellent new creature is driven less by high social goals than a vague longing to "find a meaning in life. Liberated from the superstitions of the past, he doubts even the reality of his own existence...His sexual attitudes are permissive rather than puritanical, even though his emancipation from ancient taboos brings him no sexual peace."

The "new narcissists" devalue the lessons of the progressive past—especially those learned in America during the popular, successful liberal protests against racial injustice and the war in Vietnam. They are thus deliberately amnesiac; and doubly damned because they use the alibi of liberalism's failure to relax into a warm bath of nostalgia and self-pity. The "narcissist" has lost "the will to progress," a feature of moral imagination by which Lasch puts great store.

28 April 1993

weeping that will not stop, even here, where i'm writing this, in the medical school library—and the books on brain, so distant from mind, or at least my mind—
    let us imagine that serotonin exists as leprechauns exist: as explanations—that both the discourse of serotonin and that of the little folk are real in the same way, as any mythic language is real, because it seems <u>strong</u>
    but Heraclitus's word: truth is accustomed to hide itself—in weakness, perhaps in obscurity—the strong language of chemistry has nothing to do with depression, this bad poetry, weird scripting—the books say the chemicals and the poetry are the same, but nothing inside me answers, echoes back, when i shout these words into that abyss—

As penitent hedonists of the 1960s saw the explanation for their failure to be happy in *The Culture of Narcissism,* so have more recent penitents seen themselves mirrored in Robert Hughes's 1993 tract *Culture of Complaint: The Fraying of America.* Again, this book is less useful as a piece of original thought than as a handbook of trite, entrenched opinions widespread in the culture of depression. That's worth keeping in mind, particularly in view of the book's very clever, thundery denunciations.

Hughes rises to defend the soul of the American Republic against its current foes, adding still more categories of moral treason to those Lasch had given us fifteen years before. Now complicit are feminist and minority-group whiners, the intellectually effete professors who read Jacques Derrida and Michel Foucault, and a range of other gripers, including (interestingly) the American Right, which did not do its sacred job of setting matters straight during the 1980s, when it briefly possessed the public clout to do so.

Hughes's philippic is directed more explicitly than that of Lasch, however, against those who have betrayed America's liberal, secular, undogmatic, humane soul by withdrawing from the public defence of virtue into saunas, self-help books, primal screaming, group sex and twelve-step programmes. Hughes' is a particularly dangerous caricature, of course, since his target is a vast, complicated group of people whom, with the demagogue's usual flair, he makes out to be all one and the same. The mob that's got the author in a state of high dudgeon ranges from the lazy, to the temporarily discomfited, who can be genuinely helped to get on with life by massage, holidays and such, to the clinically depressed, who cannot. The lazy may well need to hear and heed Hughes's message. The temporarily bereft should ignore it, and get on with their massages. Depressed people, even those who do not read the book, are destined to be the true victims of what it encourages: ridicule of our "weakness" and disgust at our "lack of character," accusations with which every depressed person is all too familiar.

The narcissistic abandonment of good works in favour of hedonistic pursuits is indeed a phenomenon in this and every advanced technological culture. The reasons for this are too complex and important to discuss briefly within this book. The point here isn't that Lasch and Hughes aren't on to something, because I think they are. The point has to do with the unintended baleful use to which *Culture of Narcissism* and *Culture of Complaint* lend themselves so perfectly: the self-castigation of the depressed, grounded in our permanent sense of being causes of ruin, failure, disappointment.

After all, the only people who actually believe themselves decadent are the chronically depressed, simply because hating oneself is a common feature of the disorder, whether one is or is not affluent, educated or professional. As for the other readers of these books, one can almost hear the cry of disbelief: "What, *me?*"

No, it is the depressive who turns out to be the best customer for the belief in a mysterious conspiracy of selfishness. And it is this belief that sends every new generation of depressives into the doomed search for a cure, and turns legions of us into suckers for dramatic, useless therapies, gurus, sects, self-help.

For who, in or out of his right mind, would want to be known, or know himself, as a *narcissist?*

———————

6 May 1993

*On the deck this balmy day—pruned back to a hand's
length what is left of last summer's exuberant upspring
of clematis "Lady Betty Balfour," my favourite vine—
and mulched, and whacked the other shrubs and such
back near to what they must be, in this second attempt
to make a <u>hortus conclusus</u>, meditative place of refuge
and repair—*

 *and continued the reading, and the writing, about all
that seems so far away, yet is said to be inside my head—
these sparks and squirts I am solemnly told do exist
beneath my cranial vault, yet give me no evidence of
themselves, saying nothing—*

 *but the mind is in the world and in the waters and
earth and air,*

 *the mind moves in spirit physics, fingers playing over
things unseen—moves in greed of drug company,
desiring, in greed of depressives, wanting to throw off*

> *Nessus' shirt of perpetual pain and not knowing how—*
> *moves across the waters in the body, over the wilting cut*
> *clematis lying, dying, on the deck chair—slowly, slowly*
> *moving in fluid moves under the cranium of the*
> *heavens, spangled with star-thoughts—*

———————

Even neurotics who find the message difficult love being commanded to pull up our socks, stop complaining, put our shoulder to the wheel and so forth. The Americans among us, at least, come by this love of strict admonition honestly. Anyone who learned his history in an American school, as I did—and the Australian-born Robert Hughes did not—knows that the myth of America's apostasy from original sanctity is both a compelling source of national self-understanding as well as a boundless breeding ground of alibis for modern American misdeeds.

Lasch and Hughes are not the only writers moved to loathing and castigation by the spectacle of the decay of "America." We moderns belong to "a weak and sniveling race," writes another, complaining that we are debilitated by over-education and self-indulgence. "People now call a spade an agricultural implement," says one commentator contemptuously, while another takes aim against the consumerist conformism and lack of social conscience typical of young professionals: "Everyone is afraid to let himself go, to offend the conventions, or to raise a sneer."

As this will to address and solve public problems evaporates, cynicism and affectation become the reigning urban values—with the result that not happiness but generalized spiritual depression becomes the lot of the prosperous and educated. As one eminent essayist laments: "The old springs of simple sentiment are dying fast within us. It is heartless to laugh, it is foolish to cry, it is indiscreet to love, it is morbid to hate, and it is intolerant to espouse any cause with enthusiasm."

Commenting on the apparent rise in complaint, hopelessness, even suicide, a popular magazine wonders "why, when life is continually made more worth living," people withdraw from life into the fantasies provided by mass entertainment, the pseudo-life of getting and spending.

I am not sure that it greatly matters, but all the quotations in the three previous paragraphs were penned before 1900. All have been selected from historian T. J. Jackson Lears's *No Place of Grace: Antimodernism and the Transformation of American Culture 1880–1920*—a book that puts the current market for doom-saying into crisp historical perspective.

Then as today, we find, contempt for America's nervous, decadent, over-educated bourgeoisie was a booming journalistic business, with an eager readership among the multitudes who thought (and think) everything's going to hell in a hand-basket. Because publishers were more interested in selling books than getting the facts straight, the painfully obvious truth that more people than ever were becoming more obviously depressed, taking to their beds and never getting up again, was written down to decline of virtue, a yielding to the general mental weakness called by that age "neurasthenia." "Tortured by indecision and doubt," writes Lears, "the neurasthenic seemed a pathetic descendant of the iron-willed Americans who had cleared forests, drained swamps and subdued a continent."

What the journalistic opportunists of the late-nineteenth century were moving in to exploit is the same phenomenon that earns infinite numbers of more recent doomsayers their bread and butter: the troublesome sight of more and more people deeply distressed, and their ever more conspicuous, frantic search for remedies. For a hundred years, as Lears shows, North American progressivists of the pull-up-your-socks persuasion have been rising to high histrionic outrage at the sight of a society formerly driven by high industrial production values succumbing to hedonism, thence to neurasthenia, and establishing in place of a common ethic of work what Lears calls "a therapeutic culture."

As always happens, the usual suspects are rounded up and charged with treason: hysterical women, febrile young men with peach-blossom complexions, mad aunts, peculiar loners, odd boys who must have gotten that way by masturbating obsessively, the senile together with the mentally retarded and the genuinely, pathetically insane.

And the usual suspects are always charged with the usual crimes—though in the more or less same spirit of ambivalence. For since the late-nineteenth century until the present, the prosecutors have never been able to pin the blame for the "decadence" wholly on the individual. Traditionally at the heart of every tract, there is the spectre of a collapse of cultural authority under the onslaught of ruthlessly expansive consumer capitalism. The new, pervasive exhaustion is induced by having to beat the clock, get ahead, run faster. The disorientation of the ceaseless chop and change of advertising and publicity nails consumers to the spinning wheel of fashion and style. The New York neurologist George Miller Beard, inventor of the term *neurasthenia* and, in an 1880 book, its first describer, asked: "How can we be happy when the nerves are kept jangling day after day and night after night?"

———————

9 May 1993

> *quieted now somewhat in the quiet work of gardening,*
> *and there is peace in watching*
>   *the emergence of green from water and wind*
>   *and the mute stuff of ground—*
>   *there is a kind of coming forth that is pushed; and*
> *then there is the coming forth of gardens, drawn by the*
> *sun, the oncoming warmth, and in that fall of light is*
> *the summons of arising—*
>   *i look most of all, these days, for the insects to make*
> *their way back to the garden: the sociable bees I love*
> *best, and the gleamings wasps, slicing from the forsythia*
> *leaves perfect circles of green, to paper their new houses*
> *with—all the flying things who follow the command to*

*dwell, without knowing it as command: to dwell deeply,
in the becoming of the year, the coming-towards-being
of the world—
    a bell rings somewhere, the angelus over the pagan
city—three clangs, then pause: and the wasp papers her
house with green circles in the world's becoming—*

What I said earlier—that I knew little about the public career of depression before I wrote the article for *Saturday Night*—is true, but not *strictly* true. I had read Foucault on madness, civilization, confinement and control—and, as a result, knew almost more than I wanted to know about the saddening ways of depression in recent history.

I came of age during the postwar heyday of scientific and medical optimism about quick cures for everything. Punishing the mad, whipping the depressed and so on, popular almost since modern psychiatry's birth, were on the way out. But when very young, during the Second World War, I heard of neighbours, white and black, being dragged screaming from their homes deep in the cotton-growing countryside, and shut away forever in vast, grim state madhouses.

Such a fate befell one of my father's black field hands, after he was discovered to be dining regularly on his own feces. I remember this incident vividly, largely because of the wave of vociferous, gossipy disgust that swept the living rooms of white planting folk at the time. It was the first time I actually *felt* the almost murderous revulsion normal people can muster against the worst-off among the depressed and deranged, and how wilfully blind they are—we all are—about the inner truth of depressive expressions. Had we eyes to see, we might have beheld a man who had transformed himself into a visible icon of his invisible situation, a Word made Flesh. He had become the image of the worthlessness in which deep-country Blacks were kept: entitled to eat only the worthless, the excretion of worthlessness.

I recall no pity in any of the busy talk about this unfortunate man, nor any interest in his condition after he disappeared from among us. This incident was, in a sense, my baptism into the awareness of the depressed, how the truth about culture revealed in depression embarrasses and discomfits the undepressed, into whose hands society has put the constitutional ordering of things moral, communal, common.

I see nothing strange in the modern consignment of the sickest among the depressed, right along with the truly mad, to "treatment" by cascades of electric shock leaving them numb and blind and without memory, imprisonment in attics and cellars, slashing of our brains with knives, paralysis by maiming drugs. Such dubious helpfulness is merely another offspring of the common mother of all social and technological modernity, virtually every way of framing life and existence and work: the catastrophe known as the Enlightenment.

From the Enlightenment came the special cold emotional detachment characteristic of modernity down to the present day. In practical terms, it is a spiritual condition that enables one to administer horrifying torments—from capital punishment and the fire-bombing of cities to Auschwitz—with no personal feeling or liability, since the instruments of terror and official murder, and their use, are now responsibilities of the huge, bureaucratic post-Enlightenment state. The view of strange folk as perverse and diseased, deserving of confinement, reform, devastating treatment—and often getting them by "official" order—is yet another manifestation of this detachment, tinged (as usual) with hate and condescension.

---

11 May 1993

*The sand cherry bloomed today, putting out its small,
fragrant white blossoms against the dark red foliage
yet unfurling. Lady Betty Balfour is growing so quickly*

I cannot keep up with her.

*And this evening, just before I said Evening Prayer, the
first fat bumblebee of the season visited the flowering
almond trees, knocking petals to the ground as he
clumsily pillaged the blossoms—and there was the first
wasp, cutting a perfectly round patch from a clematis
leaf for the nest (I hope) it and its shiny sisters are
building according to ancient architectural plans under
a nearby eaves...*

*The depression has lightened at last, and gone, which
seems to have had nothing to do, or not to do, with the
Prozac I go on taking, now because I am afraid not to.
—Curious: to not be able to think of this lightening,
return of happiness, without thinking of my deepening
complicity with ideas I despise, gross materialisms I
cannot abide, ideologies of power, Überwindungen, the
language of military overwhelmings inherent in this
legal drug manufacture, traffic, enslavement.*

*Another wasp—another bee, this time tasting the
sweet yellow froth in the campanula's throat—and here,
even here in the tiny place i call my garden, i am not far
enough away from that militancy, will to crushing
power, that is the sickness of the age, not its cure, nor
mine—*

In the history of modern therapies, as in that of modern soci-
eties, there have always been distinctly better times and places
than others to be odd. I count myself fortunate to have stepped
into the psychiatric spotlight, and thereby officially become one
of the strange folk, when and where I did.

By the late 1960s, psychiatric diagnostics had become more
discriminating. My trouble was clinically defined as something
no more terrible or intractable than an instance of major depressive disorder; hence my referral to outpatient psychotherapy

instead of consignment to the dungeon. A mere hundred or so years ago, in Canada or the United States, I would have been eligible immediately for the usual heroic treatments meted out to the depressed and insane alike: "improvement" by means of whip and purge. Had I broken down during the era of psychiatric reforms in the later nineteenth century, my fate might well have been confinement to an airy, sunny hospital in the country, where I would have been given simple janitorial tasks to reinforce the moral improvement the institution saw as its responsibility. As many sufferers from depression doubtless did, I would have quickly, and really, gone out of my mind in *either* situation—due to the violence unleashed against my unruly body in the former regime, or to the isolation, condescension and incessant emphasis on conformism in the latter.

When I fell, in 1969, I was fortunate to have fallen into the hands of David, an heir-presumptive to that hands-off transaction a thoroughly deranged patient of Freud called "the talking cure," a name that stuck. David's psychoanalytic convictions about the value of the talking cure disinclined him to write out prescriptions for pick-me-up drugs, or to confine me, or to turn me over for shock treatments. In my ramshackle state, I probably would have done anything he said.

Had I gone to pieces in Montreal, and sought help at the Allan Memorial Institute run by the famous, highly respected psychiatrist Ewen Cameron, however, things might have turned out quite differently. I might easily have become one of those unfortunate individuals who were devastated by Dr. Cameron's complicity in the Central Intelligence Agency's remorseless and horrific postwar brainwashing experiments.

Cranial tinkering wasn't considered horrific at the time, of course. It was Science. In psychiatry, as in most other professional endeavours, the weather-system of belief then prevailing over North America was not one in which endless talk and interminable process enjoyed a sunny spot. Old-fashioned talk therapy may have been in vogue among North America's urban,

Eastern élite, but its uncertainties, and especially its reliance on long, expensive, little-understood transactions in language, had cast it into disfavour in the institutions. Sleek high-speed cars and super-efficient home appliances were the rage in postwar North America; the mind doctors wanted the same speed, efficacy and convenience to prevail in clinic and hospital.

Anne Collins tells in her book *In the Sleep Room* of the Allied military doctors working behind the front lines who discovered that heavy dosages of antidepressants and sedatives were quicker and more cost-effective than time-consuming talk therapies, at least when it came to getting shell-shocked soldiers back up to killing speed. At the war's end, the medics returned to their old clinics and hospitals in North America, bearing stories of miraculous recoveries and instant cures.

Such messages quickly spread, and were quickly conflated into a general prophecy that fell on eager ears in a psychiatric community swamped by needy people with mysterious ailments: that the transformation of psychotherapy into respectable medicine was at hand, with chemical and electric super-cures as wondrous as anything returning vets were finding down at the home-appliance stores. The totally planned and administered life, already blooming in suburbia, would soon be available as a gift to all humankind.

The drug companies went to work at once. Among the first psychoactive wonder-drugs off the assembly line in the 1950s was chlorpromazine, followed by a host of other antidepressants spun out of research into antihistamines. But the applause that greeted these early drugs was quickly silenced as damnable side-effects began to show up in patients, and when many of the new drugs simply failed to work.

Curiously—or not so curiously, given the open-eyed belief in Science at the time—neither the harmful impact of such drugs, nor their frequent failure to have any impact at all, significantly slowed down their use. The general clinical attitude appears to have been: when a little doesn't work, try more. Which is the point at which the astonishing Dr. Cameron comes in, with his drug-induced comas lasting up to sixty-five hours, machines capable of delivering memory-obliterating shocks to the brain, and unbounded mad-doctor enthusiasm for gadgetry. *Understanding* patients was obsolete. *Curing* them—the more automatically, disinterestedly, "scientifically," the better—became paramount.

---

20 May 1993

already on my way to France, in the mind—already
on the plane, though another space within the mind
opens to the sky, the rain of these May days, and seeds
grow there—
  Ascension Day: and the day of the Beloved's
withdrawal from the world, now become too small
for his plentitude, dispersion.
  the spreading of the seed God has become in
disappearing is now everywhere taking place, a
dusty cloud of loveliness, tiny sperm burrowing their
way into the ground's womb, and that is here, and
all.
  an apparition of a bee, at last: all its beauty in
pollen-caked legs, heaved through the light spring air
by humming wings, and rotund body heavy and
yellow as the sun in this sunset moment—

Compared with the monstrously large population that comprises the self-help market, mercifully few fell prey to the heroic, assembly-line therapeutics of Ewen Cameron and men of his sort. And mad doctors can at least be stopped. There seems to be no stopping the mutation and proliferation of the pervasively destructive culture of self-help, or its insistence that we give in to the punditry of the hour.

A sophisticated depressive nowadays will find it easy to shrug off the hectoring arguments at the heart of tracts such as Lasch's *Culture of Narcissism* and Hughes's *Culture of Complaint*, and to disregard, or at least set aside with sadness and sympathy for its victims, the apocalyptic hopes of postwar medical mind-doctoring.

More difficult to resist are the new—I am tempted to write *New Age*—languages of depression. The books composed in these languages do not issue fearful condemnations from the Sinai of high moral rectitude; nor do they sternly reprimand the complainer for complaining. Rather, they *cosset*, appealing to the depressive's obsession with being taken seriously and given uplifting advice and help. We do adore stories about individual miracles.

Reading Peter D. Kramer's *Listening to Prozac* was thus an intriguingly ironic experience, because it told me what I deeply wished to be told, and what I know to be untrue. A psychiatrist and professor, Dr. Kramer has produced the most intellectually princely and literate of self-help manuals, trash reading of the highest order, delivering false hope in a most pleasing and seductive manner. I was not surprised to find out, as I started to write this book, that *Listening to Prozac* was topping the best-seller lists. As a wise reviewer has noted, for such popularity was the tome written.

Never mind that it has been dismissed with a shrug by more than one rigorous medical or scientific reviewer. In the land of fairy tale, the scientists have no special competence, and it is Dr. Kramer's fairy tales, beautifully told, that make his book so deftly appealing. We profoundly wish to believe in men and women found half-dead under the crushing weight of depression and restored to life with a daily dose of 40 milligrams of fluoxetine hydrochloride, of people on the trash heap of life to whom Prozac had given back the power to get dates, enjoy skiing, and generally get on with the pursuit of happiness.

This is the substance of the book: one anecdotal account after another of the blind receiving their sight, the deaf their hearing, the depressed their zest for dreary desk jobs. Dr. Kramer has collected these miracle tales partly from his own clinical practice, but also from that of other psychiatrists, compiling them into a wonder-book meant to announce the heaven on earth being brought to us by Eli Lilly.

I imagine there are many books about Lourdes just like this one, written with the same inspirational zeal and undoubted devotion to helping the unfortunate that Peter Kramer has brought to *Listening to Prozac.* A tiny population of sick folk are wonderfully cured at Lourdes; of that I genuinely have no doubt. Nor do I doubt Dr. Kramer's stories of a dozen or so lives spectacularly transformed. I even am prepared to believe that the recovery rate of patients on Prozac is roughly equal to that of the spring-waters at Lourdes—between five and ten per cent, depending on what you call "recovery."

The problem is, of course, that Dr. Kramer, like the sincere promoters of Lourdes' healing waters, dwells on the wondrously changed tiny minority and conveniently forgets about the great majority of sick and wounded who end their pilgrimages with nothing better—though perhaps also nothing worse—than rekindled courage to face their illness with resignation.

That's certainly as much as I have gotten after twenty-five years of psychotherapy and three years of treatment with fluoxetine. And, in my view, that's rather a lot.

Beware all prophets who deny the body, and call for its discipline in the interests of some "greater good." But beware especially those who, like Dr. Kramer, proffer "cures" that cure nothing permanently, and help only sometimes, and then only a little—while mightily enforcing the doctrines held by the dispensing priesthood. One of these doctrines, central to *Listening to Prozac,* has to do with what it is to be a person: the old-fashioned, individualistic, atomistic way of construing personhood that is key to modern doctoring of all sorts.

The healed person, in this popular paradigm, is an entity characterized (in Dr. Kramer's words) by "vivacious attractiveness," a "scorn of fastidiousness," pleasure-seeking, a readiness to lunge for "the business advantage conferred by mental quickness..." Fixing the brain with Prozac, a possibility Dr. Kramer's book tries to make incontestable and inevitable, means the creation of a race of happily conformist, consumerist, hedonistic, self-centred, ambitious Americans. I assume that this is what a *person* is supposed to be, at least in Kramer's home-town of Providence, Rhode Island. It's not what I had in mind when, in Kiev, I got utterly fed up with being a depressed unperson, and decided to try becoming something else.

In delivering unto us the miraculous tales of several people who have undergone breathtaking improvements, Dr. Kramer is making as eloquent a case as he can for the doctrine of biological determinism. It is certainly among the most intellectually crude superstitions of our secularized, mass-democratic age; but it is nevertheless the pillar upon which a great deal of modern mind-medicine stands.

The idea of biological determinism—you fix the brain, you fix the mind—is an appealing idea, partly because it is venerable, partly because it is poetic. The theory was already old when Greek doctors wrote it down in the fifth century B.C. Briefly put, it proposes that all thought and behaviour and mood are the visible effluvia of four bodily substances, or "humours," interacting with each other. (Interestingly, Dr. Kramer uses the term "neurohumors" interchangeably with "neurotransmitters.")

A proper balance of the humours (*eukrasia*) produces the usual phenomena of mental and physical health held to be desirable in totalist, conformist cultures—animal vitality and an invulnerable sense of well-being that is tightly linked with the static orders of hierarchical Nature and patriarchal Society. When out of balance—the condition known to the Greek doctors as *dyskrasia*—

the result is ill-health, "bad humour." (I would like to report that our word *crazy* comes from *dyskrasia*, but it doesn't.)

Too much bile, for instance, produces the symptoms of antique and medieval "melancholy," what we call chronic depression: a disorder peculiar, says the ancient doctor Galen, because of its symptoms of "prolonged fear and sleeplessness," "despondency," a continual finding fault with life and hating people. "For some the fear of death is of principal concern during melancholy," Galen observed. "Others again will appear to you quite bizarre because they dread death and desire to die at the same time."

It's all biological determinism, of course. And determinism—however elegantly or lubriciously presented, however intuitively satisfying—is not merely unproved; it is totalitarian. At bottom it contends that psychiatry has failed, the talking cure is dead.

The problem with biological determinism, however, is that it's logically all wrong, and can't be demonstrated to boot. I'm not denying that some link (or mirror, or response) between brain and mind must exist; that much, we know from reports of people who have had a certain bit of brain destroyed, thereafter not being able to act or think as they did before. It's just that no causal, exact connection between the body and the mind, brain and thought, has so far been demonstrated. It simply makes no sense to say that something physical, like the brain or the brain's electro-chemical processes, or a rock, or a star, is *about* something else, or that any causal contact could exist between realities as different as brain and thought, even though it's clear *something's* happening, constantly and intricately. Ending a discussion about medieval mulling over this issue, C. S. Lewis, the literary critic and brilliant analyst of past sensibilities, concludes that "the chasm is so abrupt that desperate remedies have been adopted."

What he means are desperate *philosophical* and *scientific* remedies, none much better than any other. These days, some are suggesting that the physics of brain-work may have to be rethought from the ground up, the gist being that our brains simply may not work like anything else in the universe. I find that proposal interesting, even if it hasn't yet produced results. For now, it seems infinitely preferable *not* to know something, than to yield to our very human yen to believe something absurd because it's pleasing, such as Dr. Kramer's baseless doctrine that "mind" is an excretion of the body.

The fact that an intelligent, ambitious young psychiatrist like Dr. Kramer joyfully proclaims the impending death of his profession and its resurrection as drug-dispensing comes as no surprise. It has never become a hard science, perhaps only because its very peculiar style of verbal interchange cures no one and helps only some people, some of the time, all for reasons nobody fully understands. Psychiatry is haunted by a dark dream of its own unreality as a medical discipline.

In that nightmare, the psychiatrists see themselves at day's end, squatting in some lower ring of hell along with Victorian mind-curists, phrenologists, animal magnetism experts and other discredited would-be helpers, being poked and scolded unto eternity by the depressed and mad folk they did nothing for. Meanwhile, far overhead, flutters the smug angel of psychopharmacology—humourology, biodeterminism, call it what you will—tooting a tinny trumpet and proclaiming: *Told you so!*

---

21 June 1993

Venice, morning coffee at Café Florian on the Piazza
San Marco—Proust at the table just across the way,
correcting his translation of Ruskin—Nietzsche writing
neatly and quickly in a shady spot near the orchestra
(which has not yet appeared)—Ezra Pound jotting
down statistics to support his rabbit-brained economic
doctrines at another table...
    i can remember these things, read somewhere, even if
i cannot _feel_ them, whatever i mean by that—

or perhaps it goes like this: Proust and Ezra, there,
writing, are reminders of the real in a place where i
cannot quite feel the beauty, or feel it only through its
literary mediations, mutations in time, all more real to
me right now than the paving of the piazza under my
feet, the glint of morning sunlight off the curious domes
of San Marco—
   i will not think of the years lost, not now—i will not
drift off into reverie about what i could have felt, or
known, had i been another person, nerve endings drawing
nourishment from another history, another soil—
   before me now: black coffee, strong and sweet, and
cakes—in the Piazza, a place that does not create or
"bring out" imaginations or talents absent (as dandies
and dilettantes have always believed), but does provide
a setting for imagination's bright burning—

Like the old-fashioned psychiatrists before them, the psychiatric materialists are not without excuses. If neurochemical balance is restored, and everything is *not* well—as very probably happened in ancient patients, and often happens to Prozac users—well, it's all due to a lack of practical knowledge. *We don't know enough*, say the doctors. The medication is not quite right, the dosage needs to be changed. *We have a lot to learn.* And so forth. No failure is grave enough to call the theory itself into question. Were someone to work on it hard enough, and make enough exceptions and room for eccentricities, the theory of humours might still be in use today. It's all a matter of conviction. Evidence it seems has little to do with it.

But the dosage will never be as right as we should like it to be. If a number of things can change the patterning of brain processes, nothing can change our histories, the actual tales of life resulting from depression, or reverse the damage we have wreaked upon ourselves. To deal with that history, I shall almost certainly be in psychotherapy for the rest of my life. For even were I to accept complete stupefaction as a substitute for the life worth living, there is no way to recover what has already been stolen from me by grief, trouble and anxiety. The joys, hours and opportunities snatched away from me by depression are gone forever.

Fortunately, my own psychiatrist is also a nihilist, a mature veteran of the various psychiatric fads that have swept his profession during the last thirty years. He is not prone to pester either himself or me with trendy psychological speculation. I cannot imagine his saying to me: so what if you show only three of ten predicted indicators of recovery, and still feel terrible? You *must* be recovering.

This specious line of argument has been used from time immemorial by astrologers to prove the cogency of their predictions, and, to be sure, the character traits foretold by every birthchart will be realized in some people born in this or that zodiacal sign or under any given configuration of planets. This proves nothing, any more than Kramer's observations prove anything, except that intelligent psychiatrists who write books such as *Listening to Prozac* are, like intelligent astrologers, astute observers of human temperaments and dispensers of comfort to their needy, believing clients.

Speaking of astrology and other follies, Kramer retails as solemn truth the "findings" of one C. Robert Cloninger, a researcher in Washington, D.C., who has decided all human temperament is determined by the three neurotransmitters serotonin, norepinephrine and dopamine. According to this model, each of us is born under a sign composed of three neurotransmitter stars. Theoretically, Butch's parents could be given a triaxial Cloninger chart at his birth, his position pinpointed, his fate sealed. Will little Butch grow up to be a mass murderer or a physicist? a gloomy wife-beater or a computer executive? It will all be on the chart.

16 July 1993

*Home again, and at the end of a Saturday stolen from
more "pressing matters"—bill-paying, and such—for
garden work. Beholding the changes while we were
away: oxalis at a happy height, blue campanula bells
gleaming beautifully in the evening twilight, the lovely
spiderwort thundering back, tall and rangy and much-
hated by Ontarians, who think it's a weed. No blossoms
are more delicately blue, more honourable, than a
spiderwort's, when open for their few hours very early,
when i go up to say the first prayers of the day—anyway,
being a weed myself, i am sympathetic to anything
so-called. weedy, unkempt in mind and spirit, popping
up in the wrong places, sloppy as a spiderwort, and as
much in love with shady, damp places.*

   *Whitman or Allen Ginsberg could compose a song to
the spiderwort, they being other weeds, and writing
ones—i am content to look forward to seeing it each
morning, imagining my garden without its daily
morning show—that is good enough: one showing, one
exquisite blooming, unknown to everyone else but one,
who is me, up at dawn to see it—then a weed the rest
of the day. O Spiderwort! O Campanula rotundifolia
olympica, a.k.a. Scottish harebell, soul's companion!*

CHAPTER *9*

Giving Up

4 October 1993

falling today, the soft, cold rains of early autumn:
  milk-drops from the breasts of Lady Nÿt, Sky
overarching the world in the cosmology of the Nile...
the cold milk and rain dropping on us children, arisen
from mud and ash—

walking in the woods today, leaves moist and shuddering
under kindly waters of heaven, there came thoughts, a

207

> *project perhaps, of <u>turned</u> writing, a twist on English,*
> *an uprooting of words from the stiff soil of our*
> *grammar—a writing like Gertrude Stein, perhaps,*
> *or Pound could do, and did…a river-run bearing a*
> *ramshackle boat of runaway words away from*
> *syntactical absolutism, a muddy odd current to run*
> *away on…(Jesus, the maverick word: undoing grammar's*
> *hard doing and holding—the surge at the edges, the*
> *urge and end of it, a desiring*
>
> *Beloved: in our desiring teach us the end of talking,*
> *that mix and tack-together of sounds—in our longing,*
> *detonate the hard, unhappy packed-together orderings*
> *in the I, and make us sites again, openings in the forest*
> *for the site-work from which the world will grow in*
> *its beauty so like yours—*

---

*L*ate one misty autumn afternoon, golden and wine-red blossoms in the deck garden glowing like lanterns in the cold, falling dusk, I finished the last chapter of *Listening to Prozac*, and began the last chapter of this book.

I imagined my job would be easy; and on the days thereafter, I wrote an easy ending you will never read. The portentous final words of Dr. Kramer's book had given me an agenda, so I thought—a sort of check-list of disagreeable matters to run down, address, dispatch before coming to my own last page.

"Prozac exerts influence not only in its interaction with individual patients, but through its effect on contemporary thought," Dr. Kramer concludes. "In time, I suspect we will come to discover that modern psychopharmacology has become, like Freud in his day, a whole climate of opinion under which we conduct our different lives."

Kramer's assumption is true, if trivially true. Novel scientific conjectures and technologies have always had about them a certain bewitching aroma that quickly escapes the lab or seminar room, fascinating the ever-curious modern public, and creating one "whole climate of opinion" after another. The proof that the earth revolves around the sun, and not vice-versa, had such an effect in early modern times; so did Einstein's relativity theory and Freud's discoveries, at least among artists and writers, in our century's first couple of decades.

It hardly matters that very few layfolk in the charmed multitudes really understood the thought of Einstein or Freud. But it matters profoundly how fast *relativity* and *the unconscious* (or rumours of them) became forces in culture, especially the high, pervasive culture of relativism.

To European writers, artists and intellectuals coming of age in pre-war Europe, the news arrived as a blessing on radical disbelief in all verities, rejection of all artistic and literary realism, the liberation of words from grammar and their release on seas of illogic, to float where they might. Joyce, Kandinsky and Webern probably grasped little, if anything, of what Freud said, and nothing of what Einstein was getting at. But without the fin-de-siècle culture of drift and indeterminacy that the news from Einstein and Freud seemed to confirm radically, *Finnegans Wake*, Kandinsky's *Compositions*, and Webern's *Symphony* would almost surely remain uncreated, even unthinkable.

To return to Dr. Kramer's last message to us in *Listening to Prozac*: while its underlying assumption is unimportantly true— to be sure, "science" has been leaking mind-wrenching notions into the pop and high cultural mainstream throughout the modern era—its basic proposition is importantly misleading. The speculations of Freud and Einstein (and Darwin and Marx), after all, were enormously original. Transmuted by the mass media from esoteric theories into digestible cultural paradigms, these thoughts were to prove variously explosive and creative, toxic and tonic, insidious and harrowing and dazzlingly galvanic.

In drastic contrast, the "climate of opinion" psychopharmacology promises to shape within our troubled civilization—if

Peter Kramer's miraculously cured patients are accurate weather-vanes—is more or less the same middlebrow feel-goodism Americans have considered a right since Thomas Jefferson unfortunately equated life and liberty with the pursuit of happiness. As deterministic as the most grim Calvinism, as happily totalist as *Brave New World,* it would ultimately be under the control of people like Peter Kramer, Eli Lilly and other members of the materialist cabal of our well-wishers. And we should not desire to be ruled by optimists or believers in our perfectibility. As the twentieth century has amply shown—in Russia, in Germany—such rulers are all too ready to kill us if we prove *not* to be perfectible, or are not seen to be trying hard enough.

But even at its most benign, the "climate" sustained by the new mind-drugs would be that of the conformist, hedonistic resorts into which North American tourists have turned the Pacific coast of Mexico—free of rain and trouble, perfect for blissful consuming, and for realizing Dr. Kramer's ideal of human fulfilment: getting dates. The author of *Listening to Prozac* is not bothered by such prospects, and wishes us not to be bothered—for the obvious, if unacknowledged, reason that his profession will be in charge.

In a primitive version of the chapter you are now reading, I went on nailing *Listening to Prozac* and its pop-psych gospel to the end. It was not hard to do. Hectoring and badgering Peter Kramer to the last page is a booming mini-industry nowadays, launched by his book's reviewers and continued by tomes with titles like *Talking Back to Prozac.*

But if keen to refute Dr. Kramer's worst offences to reason, I discovered my energy to do so welled up from two deep, bitter springs, deeper in myself, I feel compelled to say, than commitment to intellectual inquiry.

The first was the bleeding rub between my longing to be free of depression and my conviction that, barring a miracle greater than anything Eli Lilly can deliver, I never will be.

The second was the haunting knowledge that, while I wanted to conclude my book with a clarion-call of prophecy, I had known from the outset that it would instead just end, without arriving at anything worthy of the name *conclusion*. Books about depression can easily be brought round to a satisfactory *dénouement*. A book written, like this one, from the centre of depression, in the muddled middle of a depressed life that seems likely to go on for several more years, is as impossible to conclude as the disease itself.

I have no advice to give, no special insight into the question of whether the drug industry is giving depressives a way to joy and peace, or a one-way ticket to Huxleyan dystopia. I have only stories to tell.

---

*31 October 1993
Eve of All Saints' Day*

*night the witches fly and gather in the glooms and
glades the moon's pale ray cannot penetrate,
    night the witches dance by firelights made to sparkle
darkly by sprinklings of saltpetre and sulfur, devil's
matter...
    All Hallows' Eve, and inside me a mind on witches
flying on the back of a howling, panicked October
gale blowing too cold, too fast, for this time of year—
witch-streaks, like meteors, in the sky of my mind,
under bone cranium of sky—
    the body beneath the mind is dead, buried in a
graveyard over which witches fly—my garden is
dead, each glowing autumn flower of it blasted into
wizened, frightened poses by the witch-wind of
almost-November
    the Church says the saints were alive, were dead and*

*are alive forevermore, whole armies and senates and
playful teams of saints, friendly in ways Death cannot
touch, break, destroy— I find this so hard to believe
now, to hold onto, in the gale blowing over the garden,
flowers dead, the rest asleep and unbothered (as I am
bothered) with witches—*
    *i think to the days ahead, when the snooze under
mulch will end, timid sun will return to warm &
loosen the ground and the green surge will start all over
again—i think of it, dreading the fall-together that may
come with all that, the scatter of mind that is also dread
compacting of thoughts into compost,*

*thoughts skipping like petals over the lawn by hateful
winds—*

Like others never free of the fear that the black dogs will return, this time to lay waste more thoroughly than before, I want the wonder-pill that will make everything all right—not just for me, but also, and especially, for the myriad men and women more intractably depressed and miserable than I am. We want the pill, as well, because it would mean the end of the talking-cure that never cures, yet helps just enough to enable us to carry on, and addicts us by the curious dynamic of transference. The hours we spend in the psychiatric exchange add up to an unbearable number over a lifetime, simply because we know nothing else to do. We want those hours to end.

I cannot blame the scientists for continuing the hunt for the pill to end all pills, nor the psychiatrists for drumming up popular enthusiasm for both the project and for specific results of it. If it hasn't created a new, sparkling, popular "me," and may be quietly visiting unpredicted ruin on brain or liver, Prozac has nevertheless done me considerable short-term good. Downing those two green-and-cream capsules of fluoxetine with my orange juice every morning for the last few years appears to have slowed almost to a half the carousel of resentments inside my head, dulled the razor's edge of self-hatred, shortened and rendered more infrequent the debilitating rounds of depression that have plagued me all my life.

Eli Lilly has come up with a good product, and now stands to make many an honest dollar off those of us who find it useful. That's capitalism, and that's fair. As for their part, the mind-doctors have gotten another bit of ammunition that just might work sometimes, for some people. I am glad about that. I shall also be glad if the new chemicals help save the psychiatric profession from the irrelevance towards which it seems to be tending.

For if still resorted to by many people in wretched shape or merely feeling bad or oscillating uncontrollably between various extremes, the psychiatric interchange—whether Freudian, Jungian or mongrel in orientation—provides dramatic relief for depression only in the earliest stages of therapy, thereafter becoming only occasionally or infrequently helpful. The decline of the purely mental, fifty-minute treatment of depression will probably continue as long as people, foolishly in my view, want *something more* than occasional help, *something other* than the relationship one can build up with a psychiatrist over the years. The new antidepressants involve no such slow, sometimes painful, often boring and fruitless construction of new scripts, new ways of being with someone else. To be sure, if my initial year of psychiatric treatment a quarter-century ago was intense, hermetic, dangerous and dramatically mind-opening, the next twenty-four years of it have been tiresome. The talking-cure, by itself, has not yet unknotted depression's strangling hold on me. I have come to believe it never will. If the object of my therapy ever was cure, it is that no longer; it is instead the infinitely tedious, temporary untangling of tiny self-hatreds and regrets, the legacies of a lifetime of attacking and abasing the self with the obscene language of the depressed. These are things no drug will ever be able to do.

Fluoxetine only started to work the day I started taking it. I cannot rewrite the life-histories I have created within the culture of depression before that time, reverse the damage I have wreaked upon myself, obliterate the terrible memories, get back the pleasures and days I could have had. To rehearse and quench regret—and to keep alight my ever-flickering candle of disbelief in cure, solution, way out—I shall be in psychotherapy for the rest of my life.

---

12 November 1993

*Banff, camper-land in the Canadian Rockies, high
horizon with clouds sweeping by, snatched at by sharp
fangs of mountains snatching at the sky—*
    *to be alive now and then in Banff, to be alive now;
or then. An issue. But even to be alive then, in another
time with different furnishings so much kinder then, is
a way to try, at least, to be alive now, and here. There is
no such thing as escapism or anachronism—there is only
the particular situation the <u>work now</u> occupies, and
that work may be only the glossing of the book I write
always, in the present, the script, this life—a scrap of
marginalia, perhaps; etymology.*
        *to be alive then is the only way to be alive
now; to be anachronic instead of chronic, tick-tocking
deep time—out of step in the march in time militarized
time, each clock a drill sergeant barking nothing.*
    *Banff, higher than the world i came from, yet all time
converges here, in this existent moment and writing in
failing, falling light, the Western sun sinking for the last
time—*
        *to be alive now is to be alive then, in the past
towards which the present is ever drawn, vanishing into
that absence, into pity for the <u>Überlieferung</u> with its*

silences so different from the noises made always by the
disorderly gods of this age.
　　　　to sink without pathos,
　　without regret into the
　　resurrection of the dead
and the life of the world that was
to come
　　and in all that the dying will come,
　　　　a bell ringing in clear cold
　　　　mountain 　　　　　　　　　　*air*
a useless writing in any case, a dying and revealing,
a building of a temple for the coming god (as Heidegger
said)
　　who alone can save us
　　(and even a god cannot save us
　　　　in the ceaseless peaceful
　　　　undoing of the world

Given the general skepticism about talking psychotherapy's cure-rate, it's understandable that some psychiatrists are looking to the test-tube to rescue their retirement plans. And yet an exclusive reliance on drugs makes sense only when the principal agenda is self-mastery, or mastery over the circumstances engineered by one's lifetime of depression. That this should be the agenda of most depressives, and all doctors, should not surprise us.

If Heidegger is to be believed—and I am convinced he is right on this point—our thought and action since the time of Socrates have been mobilized supremely, and with increasing exclusivity, by the dream of *complete mastery*. Western culture can be viewed as a vast laboratory of such mastery—over nature, over ourselves, over our moods, over the unknown, the known, the unknowable and (as we learned from the horrifying medical experiments at Auschwitz) that which is not worth knowing. Our contemporary languages of everything from sex and career to subatomic particles and disease share a common rhetoric of conquest. And this rhetoric, over the twenty-five hundred years of its career, has created the mechanized, increasingly automated environment we inhabit, as well as the strategizing, calculating souls that we have become.

But with the emergence of a culture of mastery comes continual conflict, the war for the scarce spoils. Hence the vast dismay and tremendous mental misery felt by "losers" in this war—the people, that is, who feel they *aren't getting theirs*. As compensation to the losers in the headlong quest for mastery—which is all but the holiest and most detached of us—mass society has created a culture of distraction and pseudo-fulfilment. The environment is saturated with utopian eroticism of the sort found in Calvin Klein underwear advertisements, while the social machine we work and live within is drenched with sedative, amnesiac grease.

Hence the peculiar significance of Prozac, and the great expectations it has encouraged for ever-better, faster, newer pick-me-uppers. Psychiatry is simply too slow. Like the victims of battle trauma during the Second World War, we participants in the endless war of everyone against everyone must have ever-better potions to extinguish the punishing shame of loss and failure if we are going to be able to get out of bed each day and fight another round in the conflict without end.

I experience both depression and its treatment as continuous mass-cultural phenomena, not individual disease and one-to-one therapy. Depression has always been for me, and remains, a self-punishing language, a prolonged sensation of filthiness and worthlessness, of embarrassment at being alive; a sickening deadness I enviously compare to the liveliness other people seem to enjoy. I cannot imagine it other than as a constellation of images and words inextricably connected to models, disturbances, languages "out there," in the field of social existence.

Western medicine, like any other discipline in our tradition of complete overpowering, has insisted always on treating depressive patients as disordered things. It has produced a strong technical language and practice, drawn from biological materialism and determinism, which effectively reduces us to such manageable, and treatable things. The doctor's art is a kind of "radical, sullen atheism," to borrow and misapply Julia Kristeva's description of depression. Acting in that spirit, contemporary medicine knows nothing of its patients as systems.

If Kristeva's phrase seems to fit, it's because our encounters with medical power are often quite as dispiriting as depression itself. In addition to degrading ourselves, we are ourselves degraded into topics of analysis, taxonomy and inventory. In my sane moments, and outside the clinic, I do not experience myself this way. My waking consciousness suggests that I am one knot in the general entwinements of culture, a tiny history inextricable from the general history of language, sense, sensibility. My existence within this history is pain; an everydayness afflicted always by depression, but at some times more obstructively than at others. I can sometimes follow happy practices, like dance-steps printed on paper, at least until my feet get tired and tangled.

This fictive entity, the "body" created by medicine, is interesting only when warped, crippled, destroyed by other things, invasive and alien ones, "illnesses"; it is otherwise not interesting to doctors at all. (I believe the "body" constructed by the doctors to be unreal because I have never felt anyone who was not sensuously interesting to the touch. Doctors are different that way. I once had a friend, a pediatrician, who quit her practice because all the babies brought her were well, and this bored her infinitely.)

In order to bring it under the gaze of medical surveillance and control, depression had to be turned into a disease like any other, an individual matter producing symptoms that make the victim peculiar. It is a foul-up inside the perimeter of the body, *disorder wholly within*, with an etiology, epidemiology, crisis and possible outcome. It is also something that seems "naturally" to suggest its own treatment—though treatments for depression have changed frequently throughout the history of cruelty. The ostensible purpose of these treatments has always been to keep the body alive. Their effect has always been to make the sick body die—to remove it, that is, from the gaze of medicine, from the record.

Even though the least thing-like of things—evanescent, insubstantial and migratory, much more like a habit than a hernia—depression puts its victim squarely under the power of technicians whose prestige consists of curings and cuttings and helpings; whereupon the body is restored to its status as uninteresting thing, of no importance.

---

26 January 1994

all that is dreaded about the winter comes true
   weeks of intense, bone-piercing cold, unrelenting,
forbidding walks in the woods, even around town
   the disorientation of it, leaving me sporadic,
ineffectual at everything i do. adrift in the freeze and
calm of it, a time of folding down, folding within
   yesterday shovelled out the waist-high stacks of
magazines and books and old papers in my workroom.
and all that is dread comes to nest in the heart, a
poisonous bird with nowhere else to go. this morning,
an hour with dr. rosen:
   and, i told him, yes: i am back in the prayers, and in
the testimony of the god. and yes: i am in the god's
torment and falling apart, clutching nothing because
nothing will hold me together now
            and yes: the god's passion is in the torment
and tearing, and i cannot now follow him into it, be
there, co-sufferer of all the torments.
   and yes: i am in my room more and more now,

*withdrawn from the world, since i have nothing, am
nothing
    and yes: the ongoing must be done, dr. rosen said, the
going is to be done, and that is on and on, and there is
no end of it
    and yes and yes: the not-doing is part of the ongoing,
what dr. rosen calls <u>restraint</u>, and that i am not very
good at—a not-doing that is not doing the same things
but a doing of things that are new
    but in the present darkness and cold the god is dying
and i cannot die with him—but i live, and live in the
ongoing and not doing i find so hard to do*

"Little by little," Simone Weil has written, affliction "make[s] the soul its accomplice, by injecting a poison of inertia into it. In anyone who has suffered affliction for a long enough time, there is a complicity with regard to his own affliction. This complicity impedes all the efforts he might make to improve his lot; it goes so far as to prevent him from seeking a way of deliverance, sometimes even to the point of preventing him from wishing for deliverance." And, indeed, when depressed, I have found a certain satisfaction in thinking of myself as enfleshed disease, a carcinoma with mechanical behaviour but without history, an embodied transgression against "normality." When depressed, I am most inclined to be complicit with the notion that my disease is inside me.

I am certainly not interested, at such times, in conversation with my psychiatrist about the skewed cultural systems finding expression in depression. I want, most of all, to complain, to talk about myself. This is natural, since the way most of us learned to live our disease—in my case, starting in a large university hospital—is as *individual* trauma, drama, script. To hear that the poisonous leakage making us wretched is somewhere in a diffuse field, unfixable, perhaps even unreachable—it's just not what someone in pain, craving immediate help, wants to hear. Not that it would occur to most doctors to tell a patient anything of the sort.

I take an odd pleasure in imagining that I have inside me a secret thing that can appear, then be rehidden—like an inoperable cancer, exposed to the light of an operating room, then buried again under flesh and stitchery. This is how we behold ourselves when depressed—as cancers enfolded in a thin scrim of flesh. It is the way doctors always behold us. Reading the case histories they write has taught me much about depression, and about the "objectivity" of doctors who make their livelihood from this misfortune.

Because they are thoroughly symptomatic of the modern way of looking at things, of embodying them, case histories captivated the mind of Michel Foucault. The medical records of mental unfortunates, texts he called "lightning-existences" or "life poems," comprise only a "minuscule history of these existences, of their misfortune, of their rage or of their uncertain madness..."

The text, says Foucault, is their sole emergence from darkness, their step into "a beam of light [that], at least for a moment, illuminates them....What rescues them from the darkness of night where they would, and still should perhaps, have been able to remain, is an encounter with power...the power which lay in wait for these lives, which spied on them, which pursued them, which turned its attention, even if only for a moment, to their complaints and to their small tumults..."

Encouraged by Foucault's example, I have occasionally hidden away in libraries when depressed and spent hours paging through case histories published in the medical journals. (Who can tell that the case history will not be the popular literature of the future, a sort of "true" science fiction about total administration, and total abjection?)

In one of these periodicals, I discovered the tale of a "twenty-eight-year-old woman," without name or even pseudonym, as told by three psychiatrists at a state university hospital in New York. She comes abruptly into power's "beam of light" after twenty-eight years in darkness, but only as a colourless, feature-less, stubbornly opaque wrapper for busy diseases that fall under the doctors' fascinated gaze: bulimia nervosa and "severe depres-sion," though hitherto unaccompanied, curiously to my mind, by thoughts of suicide.

Into these diseases her doctors in the world outside the hos-pital had been dropping low dosages of fluoxetine hydrochloride. It did not "help"—render the wrapper more transparent, that is, to the medical gaze. The doctors then decided that a lot of Prozac might dissolve the opacity that a little had not, so they upped the fluoxetine bombardment considerably—whereupon the disease inside became inordinately restive and agitated, and began whispering to its host that the time had come to take it to its death by hurling the wrapper from a high hospital window.

The doctors, who were more interested in the disease than in the nameless package with no colour and history, spared the object of their hungry desire by suspending the fluoxetine treat-ment. The symptoms retreated, and with them, the interest of the doctors. The case history stops. It does not seem to have occurred to the doctors that their absence of horror at the quaking human wreckage swept from the ordinary world into the hospital, and not their dosages of fluoxetine, may have induced the desperate rush for the exit, which they self-servingly interpret as drug-induced "suicidal ideation." Now merely as miserable as ever, unhelped and of no further interest, the wrapper with the disease inside is discharged from the hospital into her former obscurity—leaving only a scrap of writing as evidence that she had ever existed, not even a word of sorrow by the doctors that they could do nothing for this wretched creature, who vanishes.

To my knowledge, I have never been written up as a case his-tory. I know that files exist on me, and, only to that tiny extent, have I experienced what Foucault has called the "reduction to ashes" by transformation into writing. But years after I first came across the note on the "twenty-eight-year-old woman"—merely one case history among the countless thousands that exist, unexceptional in every sense—I am haunted by her absence. I have tried again and again to imagine her mutable face when she laughs, weeps, agonizes, binges, vomits—to imagine what she is, human and ill, hence my sister in disorder and the world. I try, and, each time, fail to catch a glimpse of her through the storm of ash, blown by the drying winds that stir the madness and dust on the sunless planet of the depressed.

---

1 March, 1995

    The festival of <u>St. David of Wales</u>
      memories of Wales, the first time there, a stormy day
across the Irish sea in 1967,
      to make the pilgrimage to the saint's shrine in a rocky
green vale in the tiny town at Wales' end, and then the
sea—
      but today: very cold, very bright—bitter winter
continuing, but the light comes back slowly, filtering
through the dusty window-panes of my cellar windows,
into the dark i live in now, most of the time—
      but today: nothing like that summer's journey over
high seas to Wales, and prayers at the saint's shrine
within the cool stone cathedral—yet a little light now...
a shadow under my hand in the cellar of my soul, a pale
sunshine falling and
      then the weather will break, and the warmth returns
here   but not until the blessed drip off ice-fingers
begins, a gentle dropping of water on the deck over my
workroom, there, where the plants are still asleep in
their garden boxes.

    it is so dark now in me, in the cellar's quiet.

*i went across the Irish sea, and thence to Wales, and
thence to St. David's shrine, and thence across another
littler to the holy island of Caldey, where saints lived,
blessing the ground with their footsteps.*

*My grandmother Erin had been writing to the
postmistress on Caldey for years, and I went there to do
what my grandmother would never be able to do, to
visit the people who wrote my grandmother all those
years from their holy island.*

*remember now in the darkness, in the cellar
with spiders in the dark corners, oh male soul and dying
one—remember one thing,
—the tides in the bay of Caldey—
that weekend, and how i wanted to wade into the
spume and surf up to my ankles, then to my thighs, and
then to disappear into the water of holy island,
into radiant dark so cold in Wales, then—*

I have believed, at times, my depression to be entirely—not just
partially, as it certainly is—a brain malfunction to which the
mind passively responds with dismay and despond and anger. At
moments in which I could speak more clearly of the disorder of
myself and of the world, I have always felt depression to be a culture, in the real world—a malignantly enchanted grove of whisperings, floating pictures, mirrors in bleak tarns—into and out
of which I move for reasons I do not understand, and at times I
cannot predict.

The problem materialistic psychiatry must face, and seems
virtually incapable of facing with seriousness, is the depressed
patient's conviction that mind exists outside the cranium as well
as within it. If the talking cure has contributed anything to my
understanding, it is the conviction that neurosis is a cultural construction, a complex structure of language with a lexicon of hell-
stinking words, wrenched and debased and loaded with hatred,

drawn from a social world permeated by hate, contempt and violence, and infected with profound, furious disappointment that it has not brought everything under complete control.

Certain mind diseases are, of course, reflections of disfigured tissue and circuitry. Our little brains, being mortal, are naturally liable to the same attacks and failures that can afflict heart, pancreas, liver. All can be riddled with cancer, burnt by infections, and wrecked by accidents.

Yet if the brain is the seat of mind, as the liver is the seat of a great work of purification, the brain, unlike the liver, is a house with many open windows. Through them, mind moves easily back and forth, bringing to the body languages moulded continually by the outside play of lights and shadows, images and experiences, words and desires. The other organs presumably do not have an existence of any sort beyond the boundaries of the skins.

Only the brain is open to a transaction not merely one way, *in,* and that makes all the difference, even if it is hard to say what the difference is *between.* I am inclined to think, however, that the difference is simple, and audible in the terrors and obsessions, the distortions and rejections and miserable withdrawals into self-punishing nothingness characteristic of depressive discourse. The liver, the heart, the bladder are all privileged to be ignorant of the world. Only the brain, it appears, possesses an instrument—the mind—capable of bringing back into the body the terrible news.

Writing these words in a more or less steady state of mind, I see no reason, given the miseries and viciousness with which millions are afflicted, why I should want to be "normal."

I hasten to add that I am not advocating the view of depression as *merely* a mirroring of mass cultural crisis in the innocent soul. This view, you may recall, was put about by the British psychiatrist R. D. Laing and numerous "radical" doctors and lay pundits in the 1960s, partly as a rejoinder to the brain-blasting done by Ewen Cameron, assembly-line lobotomists and other heroic mind-doctors of this persuasion. Popularized, this vision of innocence crying out against violation became merely another gripe in the great counter-cultural nattering against everything deemed to be Establishment.

The "alternative" views of Laing and company did not last very many years or put down durable roots, and, of course, have never penetrated the orthodox psychiatric establishment. One reason for this rapid wilt was that its assumptions were ignorant. The brain is not an Edenic *tabula rasa*. It is born with our bodies into a history distorted and made wretched before our time, and is *physiologically* ordered, disposed and predisposed by that wretchedness. That is one reason Prozac and other chemical antidepressants are able to help, if and when they help.

It is wrong and wilfully ignorant of the complexities of depression; but the Laingian absurdity nevertheless turns us, I believe, in the right direction. Though nothing can make depression desirable or worthwhile, depressive behaviour can certainly be seen as an appropriate response in this deranged world. Similarly, a nervous breakdown is almost certainly best read as a strategy of the wounded self to cut itself off, by deranging language and gesture, from things as they are in a world where nothing is as it should be.

If my memory of my last days in untreated depression, during 1967 and 1968, serves me correctly, the turning of my words and acts into something odd was willed. I wanted to blow up the bridges of language that kept me in open contact with a human universe that seemed not to want me, and in which I would be doomed, static, untransfigured. The breakdown that ensued did me little damage, and some good, because I was right about the world. The breakdown did not, however, return me to a state of primordial innocence, nor transform me into a normalized, happy consumer-citizen of mass society.

It *did* smash hardened, bad communications inside me and with others, and reshuffle the deck of images that constitute the

I. It reordered my sickness so that, most of the time, I can get on with an ill brain, and in a world in dis-ease. Perhaps I am not "cured," at least in the Kramerian sense, because I do not wish to be; to live in that ignorance of the suffering world would be to live as a zombie. If I can hobble on, and do good work—and still be touched by the misery around me—I shall not complain too loudly about being sick, except to Dr. Rosen, who would not recognize me were I to stop complaining.

———

If I would like to be cured of anything, it is the individualism inscribed in me by mass culture, and present always as moralizing, medicalizing scrawls on the walls of my brain. Even after years of therapy, drugs and recurring depressions, and considerable thinking about all of the above—or perhaps because of the treatment and thinking—I find ineradicable the idea that what's wrong with me is decaying will.

Writing even the most restrained, sensible messages in my diary, my thoughts are rarely unstained by a touch of obscene self-loathing—*obscene* in the sense of degrading, humiliating and vicious. Even as I write these words, I find it hard to imagine that the wretchedness that has come upon me, the unhappiness of so many years of my life, is *not* bad manners, or malingering, or mere corruption, as my childhood in a traditional family of the American South had inclined me to think.

At the slightest provocation, I still torment myself with thoughts of my failure, moral turpitude, the wrong turns my stupidity, cowardice, slithering avarice have made me take. At the end of that comes *abjection*, a state of mind akin to abrupt clarity, and one is satisfied, as though a knotty mathematical puzzle, worried over, has finally yielded to elegant solution.

Then arrives slowly a time beyond that season of deadly certainty—an evening-tide such as this, in which I write the last words in a book that cannot be concluded, except by giving up the same longing for conclusion that I have given up for cure. It is a late time in a life begun in light, continued in blood and darkness—an hour of twilight, touched both with the uncertainty of seeing and with the beauty of diffuse radiance that come at day's end. This quiet light is enough. By its glow, I can take the next step in the dusk, and into the unknowing of this ending day I have been given.

---

12 May 1994
Ascension Thursday, at day's end

and there was a start at dawn with prayers and cold
blowing rain, an end with prayers and clear sky chilled
by the northwest wind that can come in May—my big
kite, red oblong blot swinging against infinite blue of
late afternoon, pulling string taut, tugging me along the
strand at Cherry Beach—
    the kite fought the winds coming up from beyond the
horizon, from the unknowing and beauty towards which
we ever tend—
    Ascension Thursday: and the strings, broken by Spirit
winds, did not hold the kite of Jesus' body, light now
after the shattering and scatter, rising into the blue May
sky to fill all things with his lightness, at the end of time
and matters—

Acknowledgments

*T*O reflect on my lifetime of chronic depression would never have occurred to me had not Anne Collins, senior editor of *Saturday Night*, asked me in early 1993 to write an account of this disorder for the magazine. I am grateful for Anne's counsel throughout the making of that article. It was to become the seed from which this book grew—giving me yet another occasion to thank Anne, this time for her mindful editing, sound advice and continual encouragement at each stage in the book-length manuscript's evolution.

I am also indebted to Jackie Kaiser, my editor at Penguin Books, for her careful and sensitive readings of the manuscript at all stages of its progress, and for her unwavering insistence on clarity of thought and expression; to Jan Whitford, my literary agent and advocate; to Mary Adachi, whose fastidious copy-editing of the final draft saved the book from many errors and me from numerous embarrassments; and to Catherine Bradbury, former editor of *Destinations*, who commissioned the 1992 trip to Kiev described in the seventh chapter.

My thanks, also, to John Cruickshank, managing editor of *The Globe and Mail*, and Katherine Ashenburg, arts and books editor, for adjusting my regular workload as visual arts critic during the final weeks of work on the manuscript; and to my friends Richard Rhodes and Antanas Sileika, who read the work in progress, the Venerable Ralph Spence and the Reverend Patrick Doran for their comments along the way, and to Lasha Roche, for introducing me to Jacques Lacarrière's *The Gnostics*.

My deep appreciation for their patience and their unfailing support of my writing (and other eccentricities) goes to my

229

daughter, Erin Anne Bentley Mays, and my beloved wife, Margaret Cannon.

I welcome this opportunity to acknowledge the two psychiatrists here called David and Dr. Rosen—for the practical help they have given me during different episodes in nearly thirty years of psychotherapy, and for the insights into the structure of depression they provided, and encouraged me to find. If the culture of suffering is illuminated at all in these pages, the praise should go to my authors, editors, doctors, friends. None is to blame, however, for any errors of judgement and fact that have found their way into this book.

My sources are acknowledged, as fully as possible, in the text and in the following notes. A few writers, however, have nourished my imagination of contemporary culture for so many years that their influence has become pervasive, a pressure on every line I have written.

Perhaps chief, in the inner circle of these ever-present influences, is Martin Heidegger; my thinking on depression, and many other matters, has long been inseparable from Heidegger's critique of Western technological culture, language and imagination, and his views on the project and tragedy we must live out within that cultural framework.

Writing this book in the tenth year after Michel Foucault's death, in an intellectual atmosphere buzzing with new arguments over the author's legacy, accomplishment, *corpus* and corpse— writing on the culture of depression in that ambience could only intensify my already intense gratitude to Foucault's volatile thoughts. Whatever truth subsists in my reflections on power and coercion, institutions and mass society's inscription of obedience to its madness on the bodies of us all—all of it, I owe to Michel Foucault and to Heidegger. These have been the teachers who have shown me the *everydayness* of technological society, the loom of power and mass-cultural routine on which the shroud of depression is woven.

Notes

Writing Depression

xiv *Foucault on suicide:* from an untranslated 1979 essay quoted in James Miller, *The Passion of Michel Foucault* (New York: Doubleday, 1993), 55.

a Yiddish proverb: recounted by Guido Ceronetti, *The Silence of the Body: Materials for the Study of Medicine,* trans. Michael Moore (New York: Farrar, Straus and Giroux, 1993), 47.

"another life": Julia Kristeva, *Black Sun: Depression and Melancholia,* trans. Leon S. Roudiez (New York: Columbia University Press, 1989), xx.

xvi *"Shame before others...":* "Mourning and Melancholia (1917)," Sigmund Freud, John Rickman, ed., *A General Selection from the Works of Sigmund Freud,* trans. Joan Riviere (New York: Doubleday Anchor Books, 1957), 125.

1 A Childhood in Light

18 *the dark first pages of* Moby-Dick...: Herman Melville, *Moby-Dick; or, The Whale* (New York: W. W. Norton & Co., 1967), 12, 19.

3 Underworlds

61–62 Norman O. Brown, *Life Against Death: The Psychoanalytical Meaning of History* (New York: Vintage Books, 1959); *Love's Body* (New York: Vintage Books, 1966).

69 *As early as 1909...:* in the famous Clark University lecture "The Origin and Development of Psychoanalysis [1909]," *A General Selection,* 3–10.

"every time that we treat a neurotic psychoanalytically...": "Mourning and Melancholia [1917]," *A General Selection,* 125.

"Given that a case can be successfully cured...": Sigmund Freud, "Twenty-Eighth Lecture: The Analytic Therapy [1917]," in *A General Introduction to Psychoanalysis,* revised edition, trans. Joan Riviere (New York: Washington Square Press, 1960), 463–464.

78 *"a medieval sentence...":* Ceronetti, *Silence of the Body,* 8.

82–83 Janet Oppenheim, "Shattered Nerves" in *Doctors, Patients, and Depression in Victorian England* (New York and Oxford: Oxford University Press, 1991), 5, 6.

4 Border Crossings

85   *"there is no such thing..."*: Jean-Paul Sartre, *The Psychology of Imagination*, cited in R. D. Laing, *The Divided Self: An Existential Study in Sanity and Madness* (Baltimore: Penguin Books, 1965), 120.

5 Homecoming, Slowly

113   *reading Cioran...:* quote from "On A Winded Civilization," in *The Temptation To Exist*, trans. Richard Howard (New York: Quadrangle/The New York Times Book Co., 1968), 48.

116   *"the excremental vision":* The phrase is the title of the first of Norman O. Brown's "Studies in Anality," in *Life Against Death*, 202–233.

120   *Miss General Idea:* quote from *FILE* (Autumn, 1975), cited by Jo-Anne Birnie Danzker in *General Idea's 1984 and the 1968–1984 FILE Retrospective* (Vancouver and Toronto: Vancouver Art Gallery and Art Official Inc., 1984). This special issue of *FILE* was the catalogue for an exhibition at the Vancouver Art Gallery, June 8 through July 29, 1984.

6 In Writing

127   *"neutral power, formless...," the Journal...:* from "The Essential Solitude," Maurice Blanchot, ed. P. Adams Sitney, *The Gaze of Orpheus and other Literary Essays*, trans. Lydia Davis (Barrytown, N.Y.: Station Hill Press, 1981), 62–77.

7 Wisdom and Chemistry

170–171   *an international symposium...:* B. E. Leonard, "Speculation on the Biochemical Basis of Depression," in *New Directions in Antidepressant Therapy*, ed. S. Gershon, M. H. Lader, et al. (London: The Royal Society of Medicine and Academic Press, 1981), 9, 11.

171   *The Pharmacological Basis of Therapeutics:* ed. Louis S. Goodman, Alfred Gilman, et al., ninth edition (New York: Pergamon Press, 1992).

       DSM-IV: ed. Michael B. First, *Diagnostic and Statistical Manual of Mental Disorders*, fourth edition (Washington, D.C.: American Psychiatric Association, 1994), 323.

       tiny-type brochure: Prozac: Fluoxetine Hydrochloride (Indianapolis: Eli Lilly and Company, revised July 24, 1991). The scientific and some clinical information about Prozac in this book has been drawn from this tract, and other technical and popular publications including: Paul Stark, Ray W. Fuller and David T. Wong, "The Pharmacologic Profile of Fluoxetine," *The Journal of Clinical Psychiatry*, Vol. 46, No. 3 (March, 1985), 7–13; 1990 and 1991 issues of the U.S. Food and Drug Administration's *Talk Paper*, issued during a campaign by the Church of Scientology to have Prozac banned.

172–174   *serotonin, leeches and neurotransmission:* In *The Burning House: Unlocking the Mysteries of the Brain* (Toronto: Viking Books, 1994), Canadian science writer Jay Ingram says that a good soak in serotonin makes leeches feed "with much greater enthusiasm," and invites us to imagine what might happen were a cottager to knock "his entire summer's supply of Prozac into the water beside the dock" (40n). Ingram's clear chapter on neurons and neurotransmission is one of the very rare introductions to this dauntingly complex topic readily comprehensible to layfolk.

The sources in the background of my summary are the following: Ingram's *Burning House*, 31–41; Timothy J. Teyler, *A Primer of Psychobiology: Brain and Behavior* (San Francisco: W. H. Freeman and Company, 1975), *passim*; U. S. von Euler, "Historical Perspective," in Per Hedqvist et al., eds., *Chemical Neurotransmission: 75 Years* (London and New York: Academic Press, 1981); and especially Yale medical historian Sherwin B. Nuland's handy historical discussion of neurotransmission in his attack on Peter D. Kramer's *Listening to Prozac* in *The New York Review of Books*, Vol. XLI, No. 11 (June 9, 1994). The notion of the process as one involving "subtle fluids" is explained in Oppenheim, "Shattered Nerves," 81.

8   Giving In

183   *Christopher Lasch, Preface to The Culture of Narcissism: American Life in An Age of Diminishing Expectations* (New York: Warner Books, 1979).

184   *Robert Hughes, Culture of Complaint: The Fraying of America* (New York and Oxford: Oxford University Press, 1993).

188   *Jackson Lears*, "A Psychic Crisis: Neurasthenia and the Emergence of a Therapeutic World View," in *No Place of Grace: Antimodernism and the Transformation of American Culture 1880–1920* (New York, Pantheon Books, 1981), 47–58.

189   *George Miller Beard:* quoted in Lears, *No Place of Grace*, 51.

194   *Anne Collins, In the Sleep Room: The Story of the CIA Brainwashing Experiments in Canada* (Toronto: Lester & Orpen Dennys Publishers, 1988).

196   *Peter D. Kramer, Listening to Prozac* (New York: Viking, 1993).

199   *C. S. Lewis on the mind–body problem: The Discarded Image* (Cambridge: Cambridge University Press, 1966), 165ff. See also Donald Mender, *The Myth of Neuropsychiatry: A Look at Paradoxes, Physics and the Human Brain* (New York and London: Plenum Press, 1994), especially the chapter "Neuropsychiatry and the Philosophy of Mind," 31–45.

9   *Giving Up*

207   *tomes with titles like* Talking Back to Prozac: The book I have in mind is
Peter R. Breggin and Ginger Ross Breggin, *Talking Back to Prozac:
What Doctors Aren't Telling You About Today's Most Controversial Drug*
(New York: St. Martin's Press, 1994).

216   *"Little by little..." and following quotes by Simone Weil:* from "The Love
of God and Affliction," in *Waiting For God*, trans. Emma Crawford
(New York: Harper Torchbooks, 1973), 117–136.

217   *"lightning existences..."* and following quotes by Michel Foucault: from
"The Life of Infamous Men," *Power, Truth, Strategy*, trans. Paul Foss
and Meaghan Morris, ed. Meaghan Morris and Paul Patton (Sydney:
Feral Publications, 1979), 77–91.

"the twenty-eight-year-old woman": described in Prakash Masand, Sanjay
Gupta, Mantosh Dewan, "Suicidal Ideation Related to Fluoxetine
Treatment," *The New England Journal of Medicine*, Vol. 324, No. 6
(Feb. 7, 1991).